"Gerrit Dawson has brought a much-needed focus to bear through this book, a focus that is often obscured by the narcissistic culture of our time. *The Blessing Life* brings us into full awareness of all that God has lavished on us, then leads us to a Christlike model of blessing others in all we do—in every dimension of life. This is what the body of Christ is to look like when fully mature, and I know reading this will inspire people to move there."
David D. Swanson, senior pastor, First Presbyterian Church Orlando

"In *The Blessing Life*, Gerrit Dawson rescues 'blessing' from the 'shallow definitions that involve getting more stuff, experiencing fewer problems or simply having things turn out our way.' In the Bible, blessing means 'the assurance of God's acceptance and the awareness that he delights in us.' Writing with a pastor's loving heart for people, Dawson draws from the examples of believers through the centuries and from the arts as well as personal and pastoral experiences to show how the biblical promise of God's blessing can be an ever-flowing source of life—even when we confront the most difficult and perplexing challenges. The accompanying forty-day prayer and study guide will help readers dig deeper and apply what they have learned."
Jeffrey Jeremiah, stated clerk, Evangelical Presbyterian Church

"We often say 'bless you' with little thought to the true meaning behind that phrase. Never again will I offer those words without serious consideration of the One from whom blessings come, thanks to Gerrit Dawson's masterfully crafted *The Blessing Life*. Throughout these pages, Gerrit edifies our souls with deep theological truth wrought from years of study, prayer and humbly walking the way of the cross. I encourage you to allow his words to bless your heart so that you may bless others in this journey of life."
Jill Rigby, founder/CEO of Manners of the Heart and author of *Raising Respectful Children in a Disrespectful World*

"*The Blessing Life* . . . is the kind of book that will change everything you ever thought about blessing—from God, to God and to others. Not only that, it will change your life in ways you never dreamed. I commend this book to you. After you read it, you will 'rise up' and call Gerrit Dawson blessed for having written it."
Steve Brown, author of *Three Free Sins*, Bible teacher on the national radio program *Key Life* and professor at Reformed Seminary, Orlando, Florida

"*The Blessing Life* is a love story about a love that's bigger than the universe. As I read the book, I found myself ushered, amazingly, into the transformative love story of Jesus and his Father that's been opened up to include me—to include us! *The Blessing Life* was written for the weary and heavy laden. In other words, it was certainly written for me (and probably for you, too) . . . for the glory of God and the good of others. I'm confident this book will change the way you think of God's love and the way you live life in the community of the saints."

Dan Cruver, executive director of Together for Adoption and author of *Reclaiming Adoption*

"Just as astronomical images taken in the infrared, visible and ultraviolet wavelengths of the electromagnetic spectrum reveal different structures and features of nebulae and galaxies, so Gerrit Dawson's images of blessing in the biblical spectrum reveal a rich and life-enhancing approach to a flourishing life. *The Blessing Life* creatively explores how the acceptance and favor of the living God elevates our lives and provides a basis for purpose and persistence amid the turbulent conditions of this soul-forming world, and it invites us to give away what we have received as we become conduits of grace in the lives of the people in our spheres of influence."

Kenneth Boa, president of Reflections Ministries and author of *Yearning for More*

"With a keen ability to weave together vivid stories, music, poetry and art, Gerrit Dawson's small book takes us on the hopeful journey of the blessing life. What he offers is no cliché, but instead glorious theology made incredibly practical; here is a life that is lived in and out of God's blessing, a life of communion with God that is free not only to enjoy God's grace but also to extend it to others. If you sense God is distant or unconcerned, read this book. You will be blessed."

Kelly M. Kapic, professor of theological studies, Covenant College, and author of *God So Loved He Gave*

To Johnny, may the Blessing hands of Christ ever Be over you & work through you!

Gerrit Daw—

GERRIT DAWSON

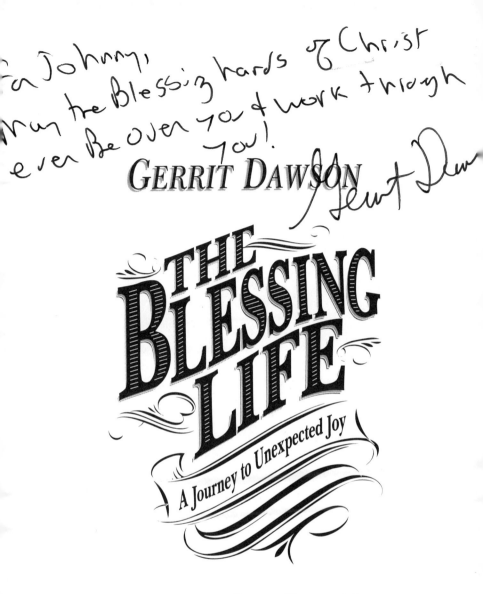

THE BLESSING LIFE

A Journey to Unexpected Joy

Foreword by **GARY THOMAS**

IVP Books

An imprint of InterVarsity Press
Downers Grove, Illinois

InterVarsity Press
P.O. Box 1400, Downers Grove, IL 60515-1426
World Wide Web: www.ivpress.com
Email: email@ivpress.com

InterVarsity Press® is the book-publishing division of InterVarsity Christian Fellowship/USA®, a movement of students and faculty active on campus at hundreds of universities, colleges and schools of nursing in the United States of America, and a member movement of the International Fellowship of Evangelical Students. For information about local and regional activities, write Public Relations Dept., InterVarsity Christian Fellowship/USA, 6400 Schroeder Rd., P.O. Box 7895, Madison, WI 53707-7895, or visit the IVCF website at www.intervarsity.org.

While all stories in this book are true, some names and identifying information in this book have been changed to protect the privacy of the individuals involved.

Other permissions: See Image Credits on p. 208.

Cover design: Cindy Kiple
Interior design: Beth Hagenberg
Images: © S-E-R-G-O/iStockphoto

ISBN 978-0-8308-3751-9 (print)
ISBN 978-0-8308-9560-1 (digital)

Printed in the United States of America ∞

Library of Congress Cataloging-in-Publication Data

Dawson, Gerrit Scott.
  The blessing life : a journey to unexpected joy / Gerrit Dawson.
     pages cm
  Includes bibliographical references and index.
  ISBN 978-0-8308-3751-9 (pbk. : alk. paper)
  1. Love—Religious aspects—Christianity 2. God
(Christianity)—Worship and love. 3. God (Christianity—Love. I. Title.
  BV4639.D345 2013
  242—dc23

                                                                  2013014790

P	18	17	16	15	14	13	12	11	10	9	8	7	6	5	4	3	2	1
Y	28	27	26	25	24	23	22	21	20	19	18	17	16	15	14	13		

To the congregation of
First Presbyterian Church
Baton Rouge, Louisiana

❧

CONTENTS

Foreword

⌘

$\mathcal{O}$f all the forewords I have ever written, I punch this one into my laptop with great regret and great eagerness. Regret, because the words of this volume are so good, the book is so rich, the truth is so life transforming, that I want you to jump right in. You shouldn't waste your time reading my thoughts when you have Dawson's at the ready. And yet there is eagerness, because if, perhaps, a foreword can introduce a few additional readers to this biblical feast, then I can't wait to get started.

Jesus told his followers, "I have come that they may have life, and have it to the full" (John 10:10). Gerrit Dawson helps us experience this life by showing us how the "blessing life" works through all of Scripture, beginning in Genesis and taking us right up to the first map after Revelation. This biblical model perceptively takes us past duty performance without simultaneously emptying us of motivation. That, perhaps, is one of the more brilliant strokes of this application.

We begin this journey by receiving the blessing of God—not the superficial blessing of a sentimental journey, but the rock-solid blessing of a life filled with trials and persecutions that, weirdly enough, is so compelling and fulfilling that we wouldn't change a thing (even the scary parts). We learn to surrender to God's providence, receive all that he has for us (the difficult and the pleasurable) and realize that even if everything else in our life goes wrong, walking with God makes us particularly and richly blessed beyond measure.

Then Pastor Dawson takes us into much less familiar territory—the idea that we can bless God. If, like me, your first thought is, "How is that possible? Isn't the very thought biblically questionable?" just give it time. Dawson's use of Scripture is compelling and convincing—and the truth that emerges brings new joy to worship and adoration.

And then, lest we become obese in our blessing, sitting back and taking it all in, Dawson reminds us that we are blessed to be a blessing. He shows us what that means, how we can do it, and his book is packed with real-life examples that show the glory—there's no better word for it—of living life God's way.

You are in for a treat, which is why I want to make this foreword as brief as possible; the best is yet to come. Get out your spiritual spoons, forks and knives, tuck in your napkins, and prepare to feast on an authentic, creative, true, scholarly and yet practical application of an eminently biblical concept: the blessing life.

Gary Thomas

INTRODUCTION

A Journey Toward Joy

℘

"Could I talk to you sometime about blessing?" I asked.

Claire hesitated for a moment, then replied, "All right, because I don't think you mean what people usually mean when they talk about blessing."

Claire and Steve Wilson's first son, Van, had died several years previously at age twenty-three. A graduate of the U.S. Naval Academy in Annapolis, Maryland, he had been selected to join the elite Navy SEALs. That January he had completed the program's rigorous winter training in Alaska. Having not only endured but thrived in the harshest of conditions, it seemed surreal that Van could lose his life in a car accident driving home to see his parents. Our sanctuary was overflowing at the funeral, welcoming more than fifty of Van's fellow SEALs who came from all over the country to honor a brother much beloved. Even so young, Van was already a leader of leaders.

When we met to talk Claire said, "It's hard for me to hear what a lot of Christians say about blessing. They mean everything working out right for them, getting what they want. I don't know how to connect to that kind of blessing."

She then spoke very deliberately, pulling each part of her next sentence from a deep place. "But if you mean blessing as life itself, as faith in Christ, as eternal life, then yes, I know about blessing." Claire could count Van's life, though far too short, as full of blessing for his family and many others. She felt that trust in the love and purpose of God, even when she could not decipher the reason of it, was a precious gift. And, of course, the hope of everlasting life in Christ with faith in a reunion yet to come gave her strength to keep going. These blessings hold through the darkest days.

"Whatever I write about blessing," I said, "has to work for you if it's to be true at all."

The essence of blessing, we agreed, is God himself, who came to us full of grace and life in Jesus Christ. Although the wound in their hearts from losing Van will never fully heal this side of heaven, Claire and Steve still live to bless. They stand in worship each week and declare the praises of the triune God. They still passionately love their other two children. Steve continues to make the stained glass windows that glorify God in churches all over. They still rally support for a school for Ugandan orphans, even organizing an art show to honor Van and benefit the school. They care for their friends. The Wilsons experience in their depths the blessing that is God. The quest to know such bedrock blessing underlies all we consider in the following pages.

The Heartbeat of God's Blessing Love

God wants to be with us. Of course, God is with everyone and everything all the time already. But God desires to relate to each one of us personally. He wants us to know how much he loves us—not with some generic love but with specific, intense, free, passionate, delighted love, love fitted to each one of us in our uniquely created being.

God yearns to overcome the separation that has come between us. Our heavenly Father has gone to extraordinary lengths, even sending his Son to live and die for us, in order to reconcile us to himself. God wants us to experience his love and then respond freely. He even reins in the intensity of his passion for us so we are not overwhelmed by it. He makes room for our reply. The Father comes to us by his Spirit, who speaks to us of his Son Jesus in a way adapted to our human minds and hearts. So we experience the triune God's personal presence with us as grace-filled blessing, which calls forth our thanksgiving and commitment.

When Scripture uses the word *blessing*, it means the assurance of God's acceptance and, even more, the awareness that God delights in us. He made us to relate to him in love. And as we do we see how God is the very life within our life. He gives us breath. He provides for our daily needs. He forgives our sins. When we live aware of God's blessing acceptance, we experience day by day the satisfaction of our deep longing for connection to him. And through each season God undergirds us with the hope of everlasting life.

The Bible tells a blessing story. God created us to live in the favor of his blessing love. So we have to rescue the word *blessing* from shallow definitions that involve getting more stuff, experiencing fewer problems or simply having things turn out our way. The heart of blessing in Scripture involves a vibrant relationship with the triune God who loves us utterly. Running like a golden thread through its pages is his repeated promise, "I will walk among you, and I will be your God, and you shall be my people." This kind of blessing, then, does not depend on how well things are going for us. God's blessing can energize us even when the circumstances of life are draining. Nourishing love can flow between God and us no matter what happens. Such blessing lights up every moment with significance. It moves us to bless God back in joyful praise that we should be so enfolded in his heart.

Blessing in the Bible also means that God sends us to extend his blessing love to others. "In you all the families of the world shall be blessed," God told Abraham (Genesis 12:3). That promise continues through the centuries. We who have known his reconciling, accepting grace offer other people that blessing by what we say and do. So living daily in awareness of God's personal blessing leads us to participate in God's massive blessing project that spreads throughout the whole creation. We get a stake in the very mission of God. If we could live in the flow of that kind of blessing, wouldn't we experience a fulfillment greater than any riches? Wouldn't the joy sustain us in every season of life?

That's the understanding of blessing we're after in this book. We're seeking to indwell the story of God's blessing love so deeply that it can be an ever-flowing source of life for us. Then we want to learn to express that blessing back to God and also out to others. We want to live in the middle of God's blessing love so that we not only have joy but spread joy. The journey to joy at the heart of Christianity runs along the blessing path written in the Scriptures. I'd like to walk those blessing roads with you.

Always Under Blessing Hands

The last episode of the Gospel of Luke first plunged me into the quest to uncover this deep meaning of blessing in the Bible. I kept running into this blessing story with the feeling that though I had read it many times before, I had never truly seen it:

> Then [Jesus] led them out as far as Bethany, and lifting up his hands he blessed them. While he blessed them, he parted from them and was carried up into heaven. And they worshiped him and returned to Jerusalem with great joy, and were continually in the temple blessing God. (Luke 24:50-53)

I love this image of the risen Jesus raising his hands over his disciples. Just a few weeks earlier, his loving arms had been stretched wide in agony on the cross. Now he lifted them freely in a gesture of full, hearty embrace. He opened his palms toward them. The nail prints were still there. But no deathly power now bound him. The triumphant Jesus poured his love upon his disciples. His lifted hands comforted them. His face shone. His words blessed. Jesus gave them a final, full-bodied message of assurance before returning to heaven. The moment would linger in their memories. It would energize their mission for him through the years. They would live from Jesus' blessing as they brought the blessing news of his gospel to the ends of the world.

This story reminds me of the place where I first experienced blessing hands and words each week—the benediction at the end of our worship service. Even as a boy I loved these moments—and not just because we were finally getting out of church. Our minister would lift both hands over us and speak words linking us to God before we left. Most people would bow their heads and close their eyes. But I would look right at the minister. I remember the light gleaming off his glasses, making him sparkle. I watched him smile and sometimes I caught his eye so that the smile seemed to be just for me. His outstretched arms, like those of Jesus ascending, embraced all of us. This weekly moment of benediction always felt both familiar and mysterious. The "good word" of the closing blessing both warmed me and gave me the shivers at the same time. Though I couldn't explain it, I knew this was a holy gesture.

Over the years I've thought about why I felt simultaneously assured and awestruck during these moments. On the one hand, those blessing words helped me feel that God loved me personally. With a smile on his face and his arms open wide, our minister transferred the affections of my heavenly Father to me. I saw and heard the love of God. But on the other hand, I also felt that God claimed me through those words. The benediction distilled all that had been said during the service. And before I went back out into daily life, it enfolded me into the huge story of God's sending his Son into the world to save us. The gospel demanded my participation. We went out reminded that we were part of something bigger than our ordinary lives even as we felt loved in the midst of the dailiness of the week ahead. God would go with us until we met again. But that meant that we were to remember God and obey his purposes for us all week. We were blessed in order to go out and participate in blessing God and others. Like the disciples, we were to live from receiving God's blessing to giving God's blessing.

Of course, in my youth I couldn't have explained all that was going on in that experience. But the weekly benediction formed me over time. It claimed me and it sent me. These blessing moments proved to be much more significant than any possession I ever received that someone might refer to as "a real blessing." So too the blessing Jesus gave his disciples as he ascended had very little to do with giving them stuff. It certainly wasn't a promise that they would have a life of ease and pleasure. All but one of the disciples died a martyr's death, and the last died as an exile on a Roman prison island. Blessing in this scene was about staying connected. In Matthew's Gospel Jesus' final words were, "Behold, I am with you always, to the end of the age" (Matthew 28:20). Even though he would physically part from them, Jesus' favor and presence, his love and life would never leave his disciples. His relationship with them would be the true, continuing blessing.

Engaging the Bible's Blessing Dynamic

Scripture reveals a three-stage dynamic of blessing, which God calls each of us to enter. Each stage fuels the other, so once we get into this blessing dynamic we are propelled toward intimacy with God and others, which brings a joy no circumstances can take away. It works like this:

1. Receive the blessing love of God. God exists, and his very nature is love. When God created humanity, he blessed us for a life of fruitful love. He made us for relationship with himself. Though we quickly rejected God's blessing love, he never gave up on us. Since our fall God has undertaken a massive re-blessing project in the world, and he wants to include each one of us. From the call of Abraham to the giving of his Son Jesus Christ, God has been about the business of blessing anew his lost and wandering creation. We enter God's blessing project as we by faith receive the blessing of the salvation he has for us in Jesus.

This means delving deeply into the blessing story woven through Scripture. God wants us to know him, and the place where he makes himself known is his Word. We enter that story as if it were our own—because it is. We will explore how hearing God through Scripture changes us from the inside out.

2. Return blessing to God through worship. Once we receive deeply into our hearts the blessing of God's love, his Spirit within us prompts us to make a return. We bless God back. That is, we praise God by describing what we have learned of who he is and what he is up to in the world. We thank God for what he does in us and what he purposes for his whole creation. Now, most of us have rather weak "praise muscles." We simply don't bless God very much. But the more we learn to know our blessing God, the more praise we have to render. And the more textured and passionate our worship, the more we taste God's joy and the intimacy of our relationship deepens.

3. Reflect the blessing love of God by blessing others. The next stage in the cycle is to turn the blessing we have received toward others. We learn to look at people as God does, and we act toward them accordingly: in love and mercy. We begin to live to bless. We participate in God's plan to extend his blessing love to the ends of the earth. Because we must overcome deep self-centeredness to

bless others, this stage moves us out of ourselves. We leave life's joy
stealers behind and feel more alive than ever before.

This three-part dynamic is what we will call the blessing life. It
offers the significance of having our lives aligned with the true
purposes of God for humanity. We discover that there is wondrous
news about God's love to receive. There are mighty works of
blessing love for each of us to take up. There are passionate words
of worship for us to offer our God. Each activity of the blessing life
fuels the other. As we bless, the deep joy of God wells up through
daily life.

What Could Happen?

So what happens if we engage each stage of this blessing dynamic
more deliberately? The results range from the dramatic to the daily,
but the joy of connecting in love runs beneath every example. Here
are just two.

A good friend of mine from church was traveling home from a
business trip. He politely greeted the woman who took the seat
next to him, then returned to his reading. During the flight he noticed the woman crying. Though he was tired from his work, my
friend knew God was calling him to make an inquiry. It turned out
that the woman's husband had come to Baton Rouge looking for
work and had been hit by a car and killed while crossing the
highway. She was traveling alone on a mission to identify his body
at the hospital morgue. She was a stranger to our city and dis-
traught with shock and grief.

So my friend changed his plans, hailed a cab and rode with the
woman to the hospital. He went with this stranger to the morgue
and stood by while she confirmed that the body was her husband's.
Afterward he took her to the hospital chapel to find some quiet
moments to regain her composure. He prayed aloud for her the
comfort of our everlasting God. He was quite concretely the hands

and voice of Christ to this woman he had never seen before. Why did my friend risk this messy encounter when so many of us would have kept our noses buried in our books, then rushed off the plane? Because over the years he had opened himself to the blessing life. My friend had encountered the blessing love of Christ in his late twenties. As he received the grace of Jesus, he saw over time how both his own lost soul and his imperiled marriage were healed. He also connected to an older man who told him that "giving people were joyful people," and he wanted to be that way. So as a prospering business gave my friend more opportunities, he entered into the joyful adventure of being available to bless others— even when it led him to a morgue with a stranger.

A world of wonders opens to us as we enter God's blessing dynamic. Of course, not every day brings an encounter as dramatic as my friend experienced at the airport. But a young mother who intentionally engaged the blessing life discovered how much everyday life could change. She wrote me this email:

> Studying the blessing life has really helped me recognize my very personal relationship with Jesus and also the amazing love that God has for us that is beyond comprehension. In our young moms small group, we often talk about how much this applies to us as mothers and how we feel we have become more patient and compassionate toward our children. We have hugged more, listened more (with two ears!) and have just been in general more kind and gentle to our families.
>
> It is amazing to watch how much our kids can bless others without even trying. We were at the grocery store last week in line, and Brayden and Cooper were fighting over a snack, pushing each other a little. I said, "Guys, do not push each other. Your hands are for hugging, not pushing." Brayden looked at me and said, "I thought our hands were for praying."

I smiled and said, "Yeah, that too, sweetie." And I couldn't help but notice the smiles that came from people around us.

I was thrilled when I got this message, because all three parts of the blessing dynamic were at work. This young mother received more deeply the blessing love of Christ and it filled her with joy. She returned the blessing to God through leading a blessing study for other moms and telling of his amazing grace. She saw God's blessing love reflected not only through her attitude and actions but in her children. Blessing rippled from person to person, even affecting passersby in stores! And joy bubbled up in her life as a result.

The blessing life is the real deal. It doesn't prevent rough times, but it works in the midst of them. It doesn't promise financial rewards, travel opportunities or even the elimination of suffering. But the blessing life is a great adventure that will enrich your soul in every circumstance.

Along the Way

Through the three sections of this book we will work through each stage of the blessing dynamic. As you journey, I invite you to engage the blessing life each day through the Forty-Day Prayer and Study Guide. Each day you will find Scriptures and reflection questions that enable you to receive, return and reflect God's blessing. Plus there will be a suggestion for a practical blessing in which you will be challenged with a simple, immediate way to bless others. This prayer guide makes a perfect experiential companion to the study we'll be undertaking.

Also, you can read more about the theology underlying each stage of the blessing life by visiting www.fpcbr.org/blessinglife, where you'll find rich biblical content relating to each stage of God's blessing dynamic.

Step with me now into the life of the God who is love. Come

with me as first we look through the lens of blessing at the love story God has been telling since the beginning of creation. He wants to be with us. He wants to make himself known in our hearts and through our daily lives. He wants to bless us with his joy.

PART ONE

RECEIVING BLESSING
FROM GOD

CREATED FOR COMMUNION

❦

I'm not big on watering plants. But my wife, Rhonda, is an avid gardener, so when she's away the task falls to me. Recently I was out watering and not feeling too happy about it. But as I brought the hose to each plant, I began to be surprised by the flowers I saw.

In particular, one type seemed to be overflowing the planters. I didn't recall ever having seen them before. Light purple petals were set against back petals of the darkest, deepest purple I have ever seen. No king ever had robes so royal in hue. And inside each flower a tiny spot of yellow seemed to call me. I wanted to plunge like a bee into that riot of color. As I gazed, it struck me that these flowers were designed and brought into being by God. He loves beauty, both in the uniqueness of each species and in the multiplying repetition of millions of the same kind of flowers. I live and breathe within magnificence! Suddenly I realized I was flooding the planter. I jerked the hose away but the wonder did not leave me for many minutes.

What does it matter that, like those flowers, you and I are also carefully designed and specifically created? That we are intended and not an accident? That we are wanted, accountable and valuable to our Creator?

Those questions arise as we take up the blessing story God began to tell from the moment he began creating. Let's linger for a moment over this foundational passage:

> So God created man in his own image,
> in the image of God he created him;
> male and female he created them.
>
> And God blessed them. And God said to them, "Be fruitful and multiply and fill the earth and subdue it, and have dominion. . . . Behold, I have given you every plant yielding seed that is on the face of all the earth. . . . You shall have them for food." . . . And it was so. And God saw everything that he had made, and behold, it was very good. (Genesis 1:27-31)

The blessing of God arises from his overflowing delight in creating. In this passage God seems excited about the world and all the creatures he has made. He seems especially thrilled with man and woman. They bear his image. Something about humanity, apart from all creation, expressed the very nature and character of the Creator. This pleased God mightily. If we might use a human analogy, God smiled on them. His face shone on them in joy as he gave them to each other and directed them to fill the earth with their offspring.

Amidst this joy we note that God's initial blessing begins with the command for them to multiply. He wants the man and the woman to join so there might be more of them. Now, surely God could have created the earth already teeming with people. But we were made in the image of God. God is love. Love brings forth life. Making us in his image, then, God gave us a share in living out further creation as the fruit of loving one another. This passage shimmers with our God's excited anticipation that his image bearers would multiply throughout the world. They would experience a taste of God's own pleasure in creating life.

What's more, the man and the woman would rule over the earth and its creatures. In Genesis 2 we see that this dominion was meant to be benevolent and not exploitative. Adam (and soon Eve with him) was put in the Garden of Eden "to work it and keep it" (Genesis 2:15). Together they would oversee the abounding of new life as every plant brought forth fruit and every creature brought forth offspring. This kind of "gardening" of the earth would cause life to flourish. Moreover, abundance would continuously be renewed. God promised the provision of food through harvest after harvest. God's own assessment was that his creation was very good. Joyful glory pervades the scene.

Just from these few verses we can paint the outlines of the blessing vision of our God. Blessing has three parts:

- The *favor of God* upon what he has made, most especially upon humanity, which uniquely bears his image. God takes pleasure in creation.

- The *vital power to live and generate new life* through loving union. God gave them the potency to reproduce.

- The *provision for life* to be supported by the fruit of the earth.[1]

Favor, vitality and provision. Blessing was woven into creation from the start. We were made to enjoy God and the world he gave us. We were made to relate to one another in fruitful love. We were made to bless the world as we work it and keep it. In other words, the world with all that is in it was created good. Life for us was meant to be wonderfully fulfilling, ever leading to more life. God delighted in the people he made. He made Adam and Eve in order to bless them and give them the power of blessing. But what do these creational aspects of blessing mean for us today?

You Are Here on Purpose

God designed the world and then created all there is according to his perfect plan. This includes each one of us. David sang,

> For you formed my inward parts;
>> you knitted me together in my mother's womb.
> I praise you, for I am fearfully and wonderfully made.
>> (Psalm 139:13-14)

The blessing news from Scripture is that God brought you into being. He wanted you here, and who you are is wondrous.

This can almost seem too good to be true. People get conceived under all kinds of circumstances and are born into all kinds of situations. We can feel as if:

- We are but an unwelcome accident.

- We are nothing but a burden.

- We are damaged goods.

- There is no apparent reason for us to be here.

- Life is just a random wandering through the world.

But deep in our bones we yearn to hear the news of our specific, purposeful creation.

I remember the day a nervous, burdened little woman came to see me. She was not a church member. She had just come into the office looking for a pastor. Her face was like that of a puppy that had been scolded often and expected to be scolded again. She began a breathless, disjointed, unsolvable tale of difficulties. I wasn't sure how to respond. Talking as I thought, I began with what seemed to me like a throwaway line. "Well, since you know God loves you, then— "

She interrupted me. "Does he? Does he really love me? Do you think so?"

She wanted to hear what seemed obvious to me. I had been raised on those little yellow smiley face stickers: "Smile, God loves you!" It seemed like one of the truisms everybody knew so well it had become trivial. But this troubled woman was in earnest. "Do you really think God loves me?"

"Yes!" I said. "God loves you. He created you on purpose. He gave his Son to redeem you from sin and death. He wants you to be with him forever. His face is smiling toward you right now. I really believe God loves you."

Her face was again like a puppy, this time one whose ears go back and whose face breaks in pleasure as a loving hand reaches out to stroke it. "Thank you," she said. "Thank you."

I was struck by that encounter. How often I take for granted the astounding news that God loves me with a callous, "Yeah, yeah, he loves me, now what about God giving me what I want for myself right now?" I can fly right over the stunning surprise of this news. God created me and God loves me. Personally, individually, deeply, eternally, passionately.

God cherishes each one of us uniquely because God intended every one of us specifically. Of all the genetic combinations there could have been, my particular code is due to the will of the sovereign God. I'm here because God willed me to be here. He has something special for me to do, no matter my size, ability or disability, skin color, brain power, tenor of voice or even the size of my ears. I'm here on purpose. My Creator designed me, and the very fact that I draw breath is evidence of his love for me.

Once I met a woman who lived daily in the joy of this news. I was making a deposit at a bank in the small North Carolina town where we lived. It was a Thursday, about 2:30 p.m., just a few minutes before the crowds of furniture workers arrived with their weekly paychecks to swamp the lobby. "This must be the calm before the storm," I said, "before you go nuts with the busyness."

The tellers agreed it would be busy, but one in particular had an entirely different take. She said, "When people ask me how I'm doing, I don't complain anymore. I tell them, 'I am greatly blessed and highly favored!' If they ask me why, I let them know I am the daughter of the Most High and redeemed by the Lord. I have his joy."

Her enthusiasm was infectious. The believer gives thanks for the true reality of her life amidst the everyday ordinariness of her work. She knows herself to be intentionally created and graciously redeemed. "How am I? I am greatly blessed and highly favored!" That is the awareness and the attitude that releases God's blessing joy in our lives.

Something Went Wrong with Everything

Of course, this woman is the exception. It's not easy to live in such overflowing thanks for God's favor. Something has messed up our natural connection to joy. Hovering somewhere near the top of the list of my favorite films is the 1940 romantic comedy *The Philadelphia Story*. One of its themes involves the transformation of Katharine Hepburn's character. She has to go through some painful self-discovery before she can find true love. In a short space of time she gets a brutal look at herself through the truth-telling words of her ex-husband, her fiancé and finally her father. Reeling from these revelations but not yet ready to own them as true, Hepburn finally says, "Golly, what's the matter with everybody all of a sudden?"

Do you know that feeling? I certainly do. Some weeks it seems the whole world conspires to expose the wreck that is my life. "Yikes! Am I actually this way? Why are people just now telling me? And why aren't things the way they're supposed to be in the lovely life I imagined for myself? What's the matter with everybody all of a sudden?"

Psychologist Larry Crabb reminds us, "Why does it seem like there's something the matter with everything? Because there *is* something wrong with everything!"[2] Our intuition that the world is not the way it's supposed to be is exactly correct. We know in the guts of our souls that things are supposed to be different. We have the ancient memory of original blessing still within us. We were made for loving communion with God and one another. We still remember the blessing vision of our God. He hardwired it into us. But many days it is only a distant echo. We know the original intent only because what is going on at present just seems so wrong. So what happened? Let's go back to the creation story and view it through the lens of blessing.

Our first parents ate the fruit their loving Creator had expressly forbidden. The snake tempted them. They bought the lie and figured that God was holding something good back from them. Now, they had not even tasted all the abundance that was available. But they wanted that one forbidden fruit. They did not trust their God's intent. They ate. And immediately something was wrong with everything. As they pathetically tried to hide their shame behind fig leaves, Adam and Eve well could have felt, *What's the matter with everybody all of a sudden?* Blessing became curse. Let's look at how this worked out in terms of our threefold definition of blessing in creation.

The joyful favor of God became shrouded in disappointment. The Creator came walking toward his beloved in the cool of the day. The sweet sound of God's coming to meet face to face with his children became terrifying. They hid from him, and God asked two devastating rhetorical questions. First, "Where are you?" (Genesis 3:9). This was not a geographical query. The Heavenly Father was calling out his children who hid in shame. Then, "What is this that you have done?" (Genesis 3:13). God's countenance had turned from shining favor to deep disappointment.

The vital power to live and to generate new life became inter-woven with pain and the shadows of death. God said,

> "I will surely multiply your pain in childbearing;
>   in pain you shall bring forth children." (Genesis 3:16)

The bringing forth of new life would be laced with the sorrowful reality that from the moment we are born we are dying. Even as some babies were born others would be returning to the dust. Instead of a trajectory of everlasting life for every person, the futility of the great "circle of life" became our lot.

The ground was cursed, turning the smooth provision for life into the hard toil of tilling resistant ground. God told Adam:

> "Cursed is the ground because of you;
>   in pain you shall eat of it all the days of your life;
>   thorns and thistles it shall bring forth for you. . . .
> By the sweat of your face
>   you shall eat bread,
> till you return to the ground . . .
> for you are dust,
>   and to dust you shall return." (Genesis 3:17-19)

From then on, every generation would have to maintain life by the sweat of the brow. The thorns represent the curse of mortal futility that now taints God's original blessing.

Communion Broken

Death entered a world meant to be teeming with life, and all creation felt its sting. But that wasn't the worst of it. Adam and Eve were exiled from the garden. No longer would they have immediate, sweet communion with their God. From then on people would come to doubt God.

At the heart of her problems, the troubled little woman who came to see me was wounded from the fall. Her question arose all the way from that tragic moment in the garden. *Do you really think God loves me?* We are all left with a longing for God deep in our soul's bones and the loneliness for his presence that would follow for generations.

Moreover, now the relationship between man and woman would be distorted. There would be no more standing before one another without shame. Love would become misunderstanding. Instead of complementing one another we would hurt each other, misfiring in our communications, bound to each other but never quite fulfilling one another. Something is indeed wrong with everything. A thorn has burrowed deep into our relationships, paining and poisoning and foiling us.

The blessing vision of God was interrupted. The culprit was humanity's choice to be centered in self and not God. The technical term for it is sin. In the midst of paradise we chose the way of death. This is why the world is the way it is.

The Re-Blessing Begins

But our blessing God did not allow us to have the final word. He remained determined to live in communion with us. The rest of Scripture recounts the story of God's plan for saving us from ourselves. We read of his massive re-blessing project to bring his lost children back into harmony with himself and one another. For God did not abandon us. At infinite cost to himself, he took responsibility for the world he had made and for the sin he knew we would choose. He designed a way to bring us back to himself. It began with Abraham.

In Genesis 12 we see the LORD[3] call forth this particular man in order to bless the world, saying:

> Go from your country and your kindred and your father's house to the land that I will show you. And I will make of

you a great nation, and I will bless you and make your name great, so that you will be a blessing. I will bless those who bless you, and him who dishonors you I will curse, and in you all the families of the earth shall be blessed. (Genesis 12:1-4)

Blessing is all over this passage. If we look closely, we can see that the promise God made to Abraham restated the original threefold blessing in creation:

The shining favor of God. "I will bless you and make your name great." Abraham would be exalted because of God's favor on him. God would be with him in a special way, closer than to any other person since the garden. He would be the father of all those who through faith reentered communion with God.

Vital power for new life. "I will make of you a great nation." The irony here is that Abraham and his wife Sarah had no children when the promise was given. Yet in the re-blessing of the world through Abraham, eventually the descendants of Abraham would be more numerous than the sand on the seashore (Genesis 22:17). A multitude would be included in the renewed blessings of God.

Provision for daily life. "Go . . . to the land I will show you." God specified and expanded this promise when he said, "And I will give to you and to your offspring . . . all the land of Canaan, for an everlasting possession" (Genesis 17:8). The Promised Land was meant to be a kind of new Eden, the geographical location where God would once again dwell with his people.

We see in the calling of Abraham God's promise to renew the original blessing of humanity. This moment was part of a much bigger mission in which God would extend his blessing grace through Abraham and his many descendants to the ends of the earth. As we shall see in chapter 6, eventually the world's redeemer,

Jesus Christ, would arrive and be hailed as the true offspring of Abraham.

Because Abraham was the central focus of God's re-blessing activity, his story provides a pattern for us as we seek to receive more deeply the blessing love of God. To that we turn.

FAITH COMES FROM HEARING

∽

$\mathcal{G}$od is in the business of re-blessing the world, restoring his children to communion with him. How do we get in on that blessing project? To answer, we will have to tell a bit more of the Bible's blessing story. Abraham initiated the pattern of faith that still holds true for us as we seek to receive into our lives the blessing love of God.

Abraham's challenge was that he was already an old man when God spoke to him. Then God took more than a quarter-century to give him even the first of his many promised descendants. For years, even after they left all they knew to follow God's call, Abraham and Sarah remained childless. Once in prayer, Abraham reminded God that he yet had no heirs. God replied,

> "Look toward heaven, and number the stars, if you are able to number them." Then he said to him, "So shall your offspring be." And [Abraham] believed the LORD, and he counted it to him as righteousness. (Genesis 15:5-6)

Abraham believed. The apostle Paul digs deep into the wonder of such faith, telling us that Abraham "in hope believed against hope that he should become the father of many nations. . . . He did not weaken in faith when he considered his own body, which was as good as dead (since he was about a hundred years old) . . . but he grew strong in his faith as he gave glory to God, fully convinced that God was able to do what he had promised" (Romans 4:18-22).

Abraham heard the promise of God and trusted the God who spoke it. He did not focus on his ability to bring the blessing into fulfillment. He looked to the God "who gives life to the dead and calls into existence the things that do not exist" (Romans 4:17).

Where did he get such faith? Paul writes, "Faith comes from hearing, and hearing through the word of Christ" (Romans 10:17). God spoke to Abraham. God called him while he and his clan were still worshipers of local idols in the land of Ur. Abraham responded because God spoke to him first, calling him "out of darkness into his marvelous light" (1 Peter 2:9). The Word of God creates faith even as it enters the ears of the listeners. God speaks. We hear, believe and get changed. That's how it worked for an elder in our church named Jerry Stovall.

Going from Good to God's

Jerry grew up in the small Louisiana town of West Monroe. He was the first of five children and the only boy. His parents had no more than a high school education. Their lives were full with working hard to provide for their large family. Looking back, Jerry says he learned two crucial lessons from his dad: how to love a woman well, as his parents stayed faithfully married more than half a century, and how to work hard every day. Jerry had a solid upbringing, but he had few expectations of a future beyond the kind of life his family knew in north Louisiana.

But Jerry was quite a football player. At the end of high school, the state's flagship university in Baton Rouge offered him the fifty-second of their fifty-two available scholarships. Once, Jerry was asked how he felt about getting the very last offer. He replied that the news of any scholarship to faraway Louisiana State University was so far beyond his dreams that he felt as happy as if he'd been the first pick in the nation.

Jerry's family had always gone to church. But as a boy Jerry was not particularly enthused about God's claim on his life. "I grew up good but not God's," he says. "I was a decent guy. I wasn't doing anything bad. Parents didn't worry if I dated their daughter. But I wasn't doing anything great either."

The summer after his first season at LSU, his coach, Paul Dietzel, invited him to attend a Fellowship of Christian Athletes conference in Estes Park, Colorado. Jerry jumped at the offer, if only to be near his beloved coach and see a new part of the country.

During that week in the mountains Jerry heard a series of athletes and coaches teach from the Scriptures about God's personal interest in each man's life. No one moment stood out as a time of striking conversion, but on reflection, Jerry realizes that his life changed that week as he heard God's voice through the teaching. The verses had a powerful effect. He still remembers the specific passages he learned that week, even though the names of the teachers are forgotten.

One of these was Leviticus 26:13: "I am the LORD your God, who brought you out of the land of Egypt, that you should not be their slaves. And I have broken the bars of your yoke and made you walk erect." The teacher explained that the love and claim of God on our lives enabled us to walk with our heads held high. Jerry says, "In all my years in West Monroe, I never could walk with my head high. But now God was breaking the yoke of how I felt about myself. He was lifting up my chin and telling me to hold up my head. Not because I was a football player, but because I belonged to him."

Another speaker taught on Jeremiah 29:11: "For I know the

plans I have for you, declares the LORD, plans for welfare and not for evil, to give you a future and a hope." Jerry says, "As a guy from a poor family in West Monroe, Louisiana, I had never thought much about having a future. As the teacher spoke I realized I had no substance. There was nothing solid in me, just the outline of a life. But God's Word was filling me in. I began to believe God had a specific plan for me. I realized that being God's man mattered a lot more than whether I had been just a good guy. God called me to himself that week."

Jerry Stovall received the blessing love of God in Christ that summer. It changed him forever. God's plan included giving Jerry a platform to reach others through his prominence as an athlete. He played in the NFL for nine years and then had a career in coaching, including a time as head of his beloved LSU Tigers. But whether he was riding high with the adulation given to athletes or discovering how quickly a head coach can be fired, Jerry's deepest passion remained reaching kids with the love of Christ through the mentoring environment of sports.

Faith comes from hearing. Hearing comes from the Word of God. And hearing involves concentrating on and conversing about the blessing story God tells in Scripture. We take it deep into our hearts. As Jerry discovered, we receive the blessing as God fills in the outline of lives that are empty without him.

The Change that Brings Life

Abraham had to leave all he knew to follow God's call. If he had stayed in the land of his family, his belief would have meant nothing. Believing the Word of God will necessarily mean making changes. The word *repentance* literally means a change of mind. God's blessing story changes the way we think about ourselves and the world. Usually that means God calls us to change things about the way we live as well.

Lisa Head jokes that the first time we talked, she saw only my shoes. She wouldn't lift her head to meet my gaze. That's hard to believe when I see her now, with the light of life dancing in her eyes and a rapier wit ready to be loosed on me. But then she has quite a story of being called out of darkness.

Childhood trauma left Lisa with serious issues related to an expectation of abandonment. She lived in shame, not only for what had been done to her but how she had responded to the depression and fear in her life. She was miserable, walled in within herself. If there was a God, Lisa was quite sure he either didn't want her or would abandon her as others she trusted had. Countless therapy sessions and strong prescriptions did not remove the pall that lay over her life.

Having a tender heart by temperament, Lisa found some consolation in working with horses. At the barn she met a woman from our church with whom she became friends. As they grew closer, the woman shared her faith in Jesus with Lisa. Most of Lisa's colleagues ridiculed Christians, and Lisa was highly resistant to this turn in the relationship.

But her friend not only persisted in talking about the gospel, she got downright audacious. She told Lisa that her problem was a sinful heart that put self above God. To get better she would have to confess her sin, turn from it and ask Christ to save her. At first this outraged Lisa. Who was this woman to tell her she had a sin problem keeping her from the blessing of God? As if her own misery weren't enough, now she had offended God—a God who had clearly not been there for her all these years.

But the words that made Lisa furious came from the lips of someone who was committed to caring for her. So Lisa kept listening, even though the gospel threatened her preferred posture as victim. In not allowing Lisa to be merely the sum total of what had been done to her or what she had done to protect herself, the Word of God was offering her freedom from herself. She could come out from under the weight of the darkness she so identified with. If she chose to dig beneath the comfortable misery to the deeper problem, Lisa would find that, like everyone else, she was a child of our first parents who chose their will over God's. When Lisa got that, she was free to repent, to be willing to change as God gave grace. She gave her life to Christ. Lisa says,

Before I was saved, I was driven and determined by my life situations past and present. My reactions and behaviors were justifiable and though I didn't want pity, I certainly pitied myself by perpetuating an identity with such horrible events. A different future was only a distant dream.

But after God "hooked" me, everything reoriented itself in my life. It was like suddenly my entire life made sense. A crude example is that when I bought my house, I painted all the walls white because I didn't have time to determine a color scheme. Several years later, I painted the walls with bright colors and noticed that the "junk" I had accumulated, my furniture and knickknacks and so on, looked astonishingly better because they fit into the scheme so well. The junk just needed an environment in which to shine.

That's how I feel about my conversion. I was not created to be abandoned or abused or depressed, but in God's environment those things became almost beautiful in the way he chose to show his glory through them, in providing healing from them. After my conversion I became aware of my overwhelming purpose in being his. That whole repentance-forgiveness thing was *such* a blessing as I was freed from my past for the first time. (When I think of all the time and money I spent on therapy—ugh!)

And it has been a blessing since, as understanding his intention to keep me his has helped me endure painful losses since salvation. Since I have been oriented to Christ, I'm constantly seeking forgiveness for slipping back into old behavior patterns, but I see it all as part of a bigger picture and know that somehow he will make it fit.

Even better, the challenges draw me closer to him, whereas before they were evidence against him. There is no getting free from this path I have been hooked into. There was no choice when he called and there is no choice to leave. He will never let me go, and thankfully, regardless of how difficult it is, I do not want to leave. I could not ask for any greater blessing than to be his servant, whatever that may entail. I pray that his blessing on me passes through me and touches others in some way.

It's Better Together

Paul called Abraham "the father of us all" (Romans 4:16). Before there were Bibles, churches or sacraments, Abraham believed the voice of God and then reoriented his whole life in obedience. His faith is the pattern for how we receive the blessing love of God.

But in one area we do not have to emulate Abraham: we have fellow believers to encourage us. The truth is that very few of us will get audible voices from heaven. We will hear God's Word as others share it with us. God will use their faith to awaken our faith. Lisa had her friend at the barn; Jerry had a coach who took him to hear Bible teachers. In fact, the community of loving believers can actually speak to us before the Word does. The love of others is critical to opening us to the news of God's blessing love.

Once quite a while ago, a woman began coming to a Bible study I led on Tuesday nights. She was known to me not because of what she revealed about herself but because her parents were well-to-do members of the community and the church. She was thirty-something, pretty but very slightly built. A spring wind would have blown her over. She said practically nothing. And yet she kept coming.

It was clear, if you thought about it, that this woman had been shattered. Somewhere along the line she had been hurt deeply, though who could say how or why? She was searching, longing for something but frightened to move even an inch beyond a tightly drawn circle.

Our group of ragtag seekers and finders of God accepted her quietly and patiently. One man who's since gone into the ministry seemed to make it his mission to make her laugh. And in spite of herself, occasionally a lovely, melodious laugh would ring out. Slowly her story came out as well. First we learned that she had spent years trying to be a professional opera singer. This little woman had a voice that issued from a huge soul. Her small frame, though, made it difficult for her to sustain the demands of opera. She had not had much success.

But that was not the heart of it. It turns out she had been married to a minister. His betrayal shattered not only her sense of herself but her connection to God has well. She yearned for the care of her heavenly Father, but everything to do with God was interwoven with this man of God who had squashed her dreams. The poor dear was caught. She knew she needed God, so she showed up at our meetings. But she was so wounded that she was frightened to death of God and stayed quiet.

As the months turned into a year and more, the frozen soul began to thaw. She was known, accepted, loved and allowed to come along at her own pace. And God kept speaking to her from his Word. More and more of her story came out. She began to trust. She lent her gorgeous voice to the choir. She became filled with ardor for God in ways deeper and more joyful than she had ever known. Eventually she remarried and then spent many years working at a battered women's shelter in a large city, giving to others the love of God she had come to know.

Even when we seem, as Abraham did, "as good as dead," God can bring the dead to life and bring into existence things that are not. He speaks his Word in the context of loving community and calls us to repentance and new life. So simple, and so life-changing.

The Unexpected Joy of Receiving the Gospel

The marriage of Jeannette and Dick Anderson was a great love story. They held together in kindness and happiness for many decades, though on one crucial point their spirits could not meet. She was an ardent believer in Christ and he was a committed agnostic. A brilliant mathematician and professor at LSU, Dick declined to believe the resurrection of Jesus. It remained for him an idle tale, while for his wife it was a marvelous gospel.

Not surprisingly, both parents influenced their children. As the years passed, their physician daughter became a committed believer. Their professor son, Richard, became an atheist. I was asked by the daughter, Charlotte, to speak at Dick's memorial service. It was not held at the church but in the funeral home. And I felt led to sail not away from the divide of belief but straight into the heart of it. I quoted from John Updike, one of the most literate and intellectually respected authors in our country. I read excerpts from his Easter poem, which declares boldly,

Make no mistake: if He rose at all
it was as His body.[4]

I felt keenly that I was speaking into a stiff wind of spiritual resistance but that those words were vital to say. I remember that Richard, who had not even known I would be speaking, did not seem pleased. But a year and a half later, I got a remarkable email from him. Richard wrote,

It is a strange thing to have become your brother in Christ. I think my father's death had much to do with it, and I thank you for the role you played in the service. . . . When I spoke at the service I was an atheist and had been since communicants' class at the age of twelve—so, for forty-six years. You may not know about atheists, as there aren't very many who will admit it, but we (as I was) are very religious people. If we weren't, we wouldn't bother—we'd just be unreligious, or agnostic, or "spiritual but not religious." I seem to remember vaguely St. Augustine writing about a spirit of rebellion that leads to the denial of God. It is only in those of us who so want to believe that the spirit of rebellion is necessary to motivate denial.

I remember having learned . . . that the Calvinist tradition expects the individual worshiper to seek a personal encounter with God. When I went out alone to seek him at the age of twelve, I didn't find him. I therefore concluded that he wasn't there. It is, of course, the only question: does God exist? If he does, then Jesus is his Son, he died and returned to life (you were quite right to emphasize this at my father's service, although I rebelled against it at the time), and all the rest follows—if we are wise enough to figure out the rest from the guidance Jesus gave us during His life. If not, not.

Last year I met a woman in whom the light of God shines with an absolutely overwhelming luminescence, so bright it is blinding. . . . I began going to church with her, as I have refused to do for many years (probably fearing that what I might find there would force me to abandon my denial). And . . . I will swear to the presence: that he is there where two or three gather in his name. I know because I can feel it. And if it is true, then the only question is answered, and affirmatively. Yes, it feels like a great joy or at least an emotion so intense that my whole body starts to shake, and yes, I'm happy about it, and we are promised that this feeling is the Spirit.

The resurrection moved from being an idle tale to a marvelous gospel for Richard Anderson. His life was transformed. When he believed, he had to give up a lot of long-held ideas. He had to admit that his carefully defended atheism was not so much an intellectual problem but the spirit of denial. He risked, as Lisa did, uncovering his longing for a loving God. After all, God might not show up or might let him down as he felt he had been let down so many years ago. But in community with others, over time, God brought Richard into the presence of his Word. Faith comes from hearing.

For the four people in these stories, as for Abraham, receiving the truth of God's blessing love brought life change. That's never easy, especially at first. But the fruit of receiving the blessing is deep, abiding joy. Sometimes this joy is "so intense that my whole body starts to shake." It leads us to realize that even our worst sufferings can be passageways to the deep wells of God's blessing. The people in the next chapter will bear witness with Abraham to this truth.

- 3 -

FINDING THE BLESSING
IN SUFFERING

∾

After a quarter-century of waiting, the promised son was finally born, and his rejoicing parents named him Isaac, which means laughter. But all too soon, the story took a deeply dark turn:

> God tested Abraham and said to him, "Abraham!" And he said, "Here I am." He said, "Take your son, your only son Isaac, whom you love, and go to the land of Moriah, and offer him there as a burnt offering on one of the mountains of which I shall tell you." (Genesis 22:1-2)

Surely this was asking too much, even for Abraham, the man of unparalleled faith. It is a sacrifice we cannot imagine. All the parents who have ever read this story have cried out in their hearts, "No! Don't ask that! I could not."

This story radically unravels any idea that receiving the blessing of God insulates us from suffering. This passage jerks us to awareness that we own nothing, not our own lives, not even the lives of our children. Everything belongs to the sovereign God. He is either in loving control amidst the sadness of life in this world, or we must live in despair before our brief lives disintegrate. Either way, we are not in control. Our lives are in God's hands. All understanding of blessing must be in terms not of what is ours by right but what is lent by gift. Receiving the blessing means trusting our Father even in sorrow and pain.

So we are brought to the profound depths plumbed by Job who said, "Though he slay me, yet I will trust in him" (Job 13:15 KJV). And "Naked I came from my mother's womb, and naked shall I return. The LORD gave, and the LORD has taken away; blessed be the name of the LORD" (Job 1:21). We come to the resignation Paul knew when he affirmed for himself what the writer of Psalm 44 knew:

> For your sake we are being killed all the day long;
>   we are regarded as sheep to be slaughtered.
>   (Romans 8:36)

Can we receive the severe blessing Jesus taught us, that when we seek to save our lives we lose them, and only when we lose our lives for his sake do we find them (Mark 8:33)?

One remarkable afternoon I heard someone make an answer of faith as deep as these questions. It happened during some intense work on this very passage from Abraham's story.

"I Will Provide the Sacrifice"

Early in our ministry, my friend Steve Strickler and I spent several years developing a Sunday school curriculum based on robust engagement with Bible stories. As we considered the rich stories of the first half of Genesis, we felt moved (with all the confidence, energy and foolhardiness of youth) to write a Genesis musical, called Roots and Promises. We worked and worked until we were exceedingly proud of the set of songs we'd developed—which were of suspect quality. Several years passed and the project was shelved.

But one day a musician friend named Rhonda Smith was at our house. She was sitting at our piano and happened to notice one of the sheets from *Roots and Promises*. "I can fix this," she said simply. In fact, she was excited by the prospect of creating a fusion between Bible study, worship and the usual musical.

For a couple more years we worked on and off. When Steve came to town, we'd spend hours in Rhonda's basement trying to express the meaning of these stories musically. The finale was to be the story of the sacrifice of Isaac, with his dramatic rescue at the final seconds leading to a revealing of Jesus Christ, who himself would provide the sacrifice needed to restore humanity. The music would have to move from the quiet despair of Abraham's journey up Mount Moriah to the desperation of Abraham lifting the knife to the immense relief of the angel's appearance before ending in the triumph of Jesus. For the most part Rhonda was our constant encourager, always confident she could upgrade our efforts. But when it came to the music for this story, she simply hated it. "It doesn't work," she declared. And then she would get us to work on other parts of the musical.

Finally, though, everything was complete except this story and the finale. We'd write words, hum tunes, talk it out. But the transitions between one mood and the next weren't coming. Everything sounded trite. "I don't want to do this part," she would declare.

Rhonda had lost a young son in a freak car accident several years earlier, and their loving family had not been the same afterward. This story cut dangerously close to the bone of that loss. She knew it; Steve knew it; I knew it. We also knew that without the account of the sacrifice of Isaac, the story of Genesis and thus the story of our redemption could not be told. Rhonda tried as hard as she could to play into it, to play through it, to connect the story lines. But it wouldn't work and she didn't want it to work. She was mad. Still we urged her on, and to her credit she kept trying.

One afternoon at the piano she stopped playing and burst into tears. Was she frustrated over the music? No, it was much more. She looked at me and asked, "Why did God take my baby? Why did he take my son? And why won't my husband talk to me about it? Why did he just shut down? Why? Why did God do this?" She sobbed. Steve and I sat there, stunned. What was there to say? There is no adequate reply to such pain.

After a few minutes Rhonda turned back toward the piano. She began to play. The music swept up the words we imagined Abraham had prayed. Somber sadness: "Oh my God! How can I give up Isaac? You are the Father of my son! Is there no other way? How can you keep your promise if he's dead?"

Seamlessly came the first transition. The piano thundered with Abraham's cry of faith, "Yet not my will but thine!"

Faith turned to anger as she sang the lyrics: "I end his life now at your word. Did you think I would withhold him? You've betrayed your promises! You lied! So take him! Take him!" It was horrifying. The grieving mother entered the faithfulness of Abraham and offered her son to God with the same passionate rage.

Then Rhonda suddenly made that piano sound like a distant horn carrying on the wind the angel voice. "Abraham! Stay your hand. Since your love is sure, the promise will endure. My own Son will secure, Abraham!"

Suddenly transitions that had been blocked came instantly. The music began to rise. Passion leapt through Rhonda's fingers. In the world of everyday sight we were just three people sitting at a piano in a basement. But in another world, cymbals were clashing. Strings were soaring. Angels were singing. And all of us were weeping. Rhonda connected the story of Abraham's sacrifice of Isaac to the gospel of God giving his only begotten Son. She sang God's words: "I'll make a way. I'll give my Son. I'll provide the sacrifice, my own Son for the world. Come beloved Abraham, your gift, Isaac, sounds forth my laughter. I call home my little sheep. They know my voice. I am the way. I am the life. I'll provide the sacrifice, my own Son for the world."

I don't know if we made a lasting contribution to church music or not. I do know that that afternoon a mother poured her loss into God's Word. She raged into it with defiant faith, and the story was strong enough to contain her grief. What's more, the Holy Spirit through the story transformed her pain. The grace of Christ who brings eternal life filled her heart. Years later that marriage and that family are healthy and healing.

I suspect the people of Israel were haunted for centuries by this story of the sacrifice of Isaac. Of course they could see God's dramatic rescue and provision of the sacrifice for the altar. But only in the coming of Jesus could it truly make sense. God never demanded what he himself was not willing to give. God himself provided "the Lamb of God, who takes away the sin of the world" (John 1:29). He would give his Son, his only son whom he loves, to be the sacrifice that would save us. This is the bedrock truth that causes us to find not only meaning but joy in our suffering.

Firmly in His Grip

Susie Tucker is one of my wife's closest friends. Her husband has been an elder for years, and the Tuckers are a much beloved family in our church. Susie has always been the image of health, so the sudden diagnosis of stage four ovarian cancer overwhelmed everyone. A year and a half later she would stand before a packed room at a women's luncheon and declare, "The Lord has taught me that I can experience joy in his presence, even in the midst of these difficult circumstances." But the early days, Susie says, were a battle for her mind:

> I can remember packing to go to the hospital to have fluid drained from around my lung, and it hit me—this was com-

pletely out of my control. I just lay on the bathroom floor, staring at the ceiling, crying out to the Lord. I wanted to lock the doors, close the drapes and hide—I just wanted to sit, soak and sour in my situation.

The enemy was trying to get a foothold on my thoughts and put distance and doubt between me and God. That would not help my healing, nor my family. I needed to turn to the Lord, block the enemy and not focus on the *why*'s and *what-if*'s but on the *what-now*'s. The Lord began using all of you to aid me in this struggle as you reflected his love to me and my family. You loved us and sustained us through your prayers, calls, emails, cards, hugs, tears and food—we began to feel his presence through all of you.

In those days a phrase came to Susie in a way that shows how interconnected Christ's people are in the blessing life. My daughter went to visit a woman in a nursing home who had been struck down with a tragic heart attack. When she left my daughter pinned a note on the bulletin board signed, "In his grip." Susie also went to see this woman, saw my daughter's note and was taken with the phrase. But she did not know until a few weeks later how this simple affirmation would come to sustain her.

As the weeks of radical treatment went on, I began releasing my desire for control that was holding me in bondage. I began experiencing a peace that I know can come only from God. The peace, joy and calmness I felt were not from any real change in my circumstances but from watching God show up in my circumstances. He is the one true source of peace and joy.

As with all trials and challenges, sleepless nights came with the territory. In the dark of night some of the toughest battles for our mind are fought, but also some of the Lord's most tender teaching moments can occur. One night I was praying a loose version of Ephesians 3:16-18: "And I pray that you, being rooted and established in love, may have power . . . to grasp how wide and long and high and deep is the love of Christ."

That was it! That was what he had been trying to show me all along—how much he loves me without condition. Not when I get it all together, not based on performance or works, but just as I am, even broken and weak. As I began to reflect on the many blessings in my life, the many ways he had prepared the way for me to face this battle, it became apparent that he did not just start loving me tonight; he had always loved me.

Even Susie's skeptical oncologist pointed heavenward when she entered remission. Not expected to live more than a few months, Susie rejoices now in the full lives of her husband, three children and even a new grandson—nearly three years after her diagnosis!

I now more fully understand how critical my choice is as to where my focus is—on God or my circumstances—to recognize and quickly correct when I get out of focus, to live my life in the joy of his presence. May I challenge each of you to be more aware of where your daily focus is, to savor each moment, to look for him, his blessing and his joy in every circumstance. Each new day is truly a gift; there is no guarantee as to what tomorrow may bring. I still do not know what my future holds, but I do know I am firmly in the grip of the one who holds my future—and to him be all the praise and glory and honor!

We receive the blessing of God's love as we look away from ourselves to gaze steadily on the only one who is in control, whom we determine to trust no matter what.

Bruising Blessing

Of course, not everyone who focuses on Christ sees life work out as they hope. Not everyone who prays hard gets healed from cancer. Not everyone who is faithful escapes the thousands of other ways to suffer in this world. But even dying does not close the channel to entering sweet communion with our God.

Recently while I was researching for a sermon, I stumbled on an extraordinary blog called "Sovereign Sanctifying Scars." It was the last journal entry of a young married woman who had been battling melanoma for two years. The blog began with an update on her condition, and her writing was laced with hopefulness, humor and an undying spirit despite a body that was dying. She considered that suffering physically was actually an advantage in fulfilling Paul's command that we offer our bodies "as a living sacrifice, holy and acceptable to God" (Romans 12:1). Cancers make us acutely aware that we are never really in control of what happens in life. So the disease makes it easier to turn over the steering wheel to God. She understood in her gut Paul's words that "you are not your own, for you were bought with a price. So glorify God in your body" (1 Corinthians 6:19-20).

Then she described just how yielded her illness forced her to be, and the joy that resulted from accepting that position. Her skin was full of scars and bruises from the devices used to deliver chemotherapy. Her head was bald. But instead of seeing these marks as signs of her disease, she saw them as badges of God's faithfulness! Just being able to note how the treatments had marred her youthful skin proved that she was still alive, still fighting, and thus that God was still caring for her. What she wrote next just blew me away:

> What if we all began to view our suffering, be it physical, emotional, or relational, as a Bruising Blessing, a Severe Mercy—our scars, wheelchairs, bald heads . . . all reminding

us of God's sovereignty?!?! Yes, when we live our lives in complete submission to our creator we can look at each and every scar as a Sovereign, Sanctifying Scar. A scar that, because of God's complete sovereignty and his ability and desire to rid us of our sin, helps to lead us into the enjoyment of having a right relationship with God. Therein lies the true blessing of being bruised. Each blessing is found amidst the deep, indescribable relationship that develops between you and God as you trust in him.

That faith transformed the way she considered her tattered body. Far from being ashamed of her scars and bruises, this young mother became proud of them. Each one bore witness to the blessing of God's provision. And each wound linked her to the wounds of Christ. She found a deep connection to the God who took up our flesh and blood in order to give over his body to suffering for our sake.

So she concluded,

> I have become quite proud of my scars—they are a direct representation of the glory that is to be revealed. They are a sign of hope. . . . Think of all the glory that came from Jesus' scars. The holes in his hands and feet are reminders that we have been redeemed, saved! Be proud of your scars, whether they are visible, physical scars or hidden, emotional scars. Our suffering is our glory.[5]

This faithful woman died just a few months later. The service celebrating her life was full of praise to the God who became man, who in Jesus "has borne our griefs and carried our sorrows" (Isaiah 53:4). The comments left by friends on the blog site indicated a huge community of people trusting Jesus all the more because of this young family's faith. Out of suffering still arises great blessing.

Suffering is not a barrier to experiencing the blessing love of

God. In fact, just the opposite is often true. After the initial shock
of the difficulty, a peace arises within us. A deeper communion
grows between us and our blessing God—even when it doesn't involve a healing, a victory or a great success. As this young woman
wrote, the blessings may include a bruising, but the scars are sanctifying. We would wish these sufferings on no one. We can never
chipperly urge someone to cheer up because they are being so
blessed. But we can add our voice to the witness of God's people
through the ages. He meets us with his presence. He sustains us
with the assurance of his sovereignty. He replies to the groaning of
a world crushed by death and illness, setbacks, accidents and despair: "What then shall we say to these things? If God is for us,
who can be against us? He who did not spare his own Son but gave
him up for us all, how will he not also with him graciously give us
all things?" (Romans 8:31-32).

Sometimes, too, our blessing God surprises us with hope through
ways we would never suspect. I could never have written up a story
as amazing as the one below if it hadn't actually happened.

Casting the Way

One Christmas Eve, a mother felt that she had died along with her
son. Anne Starnes was in her bedroom watching the window because there was nothing else to watch. She could not keep her
mind on any book, television show or even conversation for more
than a second. The winter drizzle ran across the window. She
watched the drops race each other down the cold pane. They sped,
those beautiful individual drops, toward the nothingness of the
puddle on the sill that was spilling away onto the ground. The
drops, like life, just ran away too fast and were lost.

As Anne stared blankly out the window she noticed the bur-
gundy Buick drive down the cul de sac toward her house, then turn
around and drive off. Wrong turn. No through street. Everybody

makes mistakes. A half-hour later, the car came down the street again. It drove slowly toward her house, stopped, then started again and left. That was odd—not many people make the same mistake twice, unless it's Christmas Eve and you have a package to deliver and don't know where you're going. "I don't know where I'm going either," thought the mother, "except I know I'm not going to church. For the first time in thirty years, I know I won't be at any Christmas Eve service tonight—and maybe not ever again."

Anne lay in a mound of pillows and blankets. If only they would swallow her up and this pain could be no more, this wretched holiday could be over, this misery averted. The house was quiet when she heard the sound of tires hissing on puddles outside the house. It was that car again. This time it stopped in front of the house and the driver turned the engine off. A woman got out, wearing a bright yellow raincoat. She had a tiny package in her hand. She walked shyly toward the front door. The bell rang.

"I'm not answering it," Anne thought. "There's no one else here, I'm not expecting company and I'm not up for strangers." The bell rang again. She peeked out at the woman in the yellow raincoat. The coat ended in even brighter red patent-leather boots. She seemed like an elf, a picture of cheer on a dreary day. Anne thought about the number of times the woman had driven down the street. She thought about the stranger standing in the cold at her door. Curiosity and years of habit in graciousness overcame her reluctance. She threw on a robe, went down the stairs and opened the door.

A soft, gentle voice said, "I'm sorry to bother you. I know you don't know me. But my name is Nolita Waycaster, and I believe God has told me to come see you."

The mother looked at her. Should she shut the door? This woman didn't seem crazy. She seemed sincere—and frightened. Her face was gentle and pretty; her blonde hair fell onto the yellow of her raincoat. She seemed almost like an angel. She spoke again.

"I didn't want to come. I've been avoiding it for days. But God just kept telling me to come see you. I tried two times earlier today and didn't have the courage. But I had to see you. Our sons knew each other."

A mother's heart was speaking to another mother's heart and though the women had never met each other, a tie was binding them together. Anne invited Mrs. Waycaster into her home on Christmas Eve afternoon.

Mrs. Waycaster offered her the little package she had in her hand. It was a tiny music box. "It's not much," she said. "There's a little prism inside. It reminded me of the light that shines in the darkness. And that's what God wanted me to tell you. There is a light in the dark, and it is shining for you and your son."

The mother took the box. She opened it, expecting a standard Christmas carol. Instead the box played, in a very simple way, Handel's Hallelujah Chorus. A chill ran through her. How could this Nolita Waycaster have known that the Hallelujah Chorus was a bond she had shared with her son for years? It was their favorite music, and every year on Christmas Eve when they heard it they felt close. No matter what had been going on, when the Chorus was sung, all was well.

"Won't you sit down? You said our sons knew each other?"

Mrs. Waycaster began her story. "Yes, they knew each other in school. My son spoke of knowing yours. What I wanted to tell you is that earlier this year, for many days, I thought I had lost my son, too. Last spring he came to tell me that he and his girlfriend were expecting a baby. They weren't married. I was shocked. And angry. My husband and I told him that no child of ours could behave that way. He wasn't welcome in our home. Didn't he understand that we are a churchgoing family? We cut him off.

"Some people might say we were using tough love to teach him about consequences. I think now that we were more worried about ourselves and our reputation than our son. We didn't speak to him for months. Then, in the summer, he was in a terrible car accident. My son fell into a deep coma. There was little hope he would ever awaken. All our judgments suddenly seemed insignificant. We had lost our son, and he lay there not knowing how much we loved him, that we really did care, that we would always love him. I even began to think he had that accident because of me. Every hour of every day of those weeks was a burning fire in my soul."

"Did you lose him?" Anne asked.

"It was nothing less than a miracle," Mrs. Waycaster replied. "He woke up and was given back to us. A second chance. I know that you won't have the chance we got. I'm not trying to rub that in. You see, I know what kind of parents you were. Your son knew he had your love, your pride, your approval. My boy told me that when he talked to your son, he wished he had parents like you. I know you can't have him back. I have felt that feeling. I have walked in that darkness. Only in my darkness there was the horror of not speaking my love until it was too late—you have the comfort of knowing that you did speak your love. And that's what God wanted me to say. There is a light in this darkness. There is light in this prism. Think of that when you open the box."

Soon Mrs. Waycaster was gone, driving off in the December gloom, leaving the little music box and her story behind. Waycaster—the caster of the way. Shining a light on a path that passes through the valley of the shadow.

The grieving mother sat for a long time holding the box long after the music had wound down. Anne looked at the prism. It was an odd thought: the light was inside the Hallelujah Chorus. Her husband, Tom, was surprised when he returned home and his wife said, "Let's go to church tonight. I want to go."

They slipped in late and sat where few could see them. They made it all the way through to the Hallelujah Chorus. Their son's

favorite part. How could they stand it? He felt so far away from
them, so distant from ever being together with them in church
again. And yet how could they not stand it? For at the very same
time their son felt close, like he was right there with them. And
they knew it would not be the last time they stood together to
worship God.

"There is a light," the waycaster had said, "that shines in the
darkness. That's what God wanted me to tell you." Words from
Scripture set to music in the famous chorus soared through her as
she received the blessing: "The kingdom of this earth is become
the kingdom of our God, and of his Christ! And he shall reign for
ever and ever. King of kings, and Lord of lords. Hallelujah."

ADOPTED INTO BLESSING

c✒ා

*H*aving tested Abraham to the depths and found him faithful, once more God reaffirmed his blessing promise, this time speaking far into the future a vision of glorious restoration for his children:

> By myself I have sworn, declares the LORD, because you have done this and have not withheld your son, your only son, I will surely bless you, and I will surely multiply your offspring as the stars of heaven and as the sand that is on the seashore. And your offspring shall possess the gate of his enemies, and in your offspring shall all the nations of the earth be blessed, because you have obeyed my voice. (Genesis 22:15-19)

Centuries later, the apostle Paul would interpret these lovely verses in light of the coming of Jesus Christ. He notes a curious quirk in how they were written. By the end of this blessing, the Hebrew word translated as "offspring" has switched to a singular instead of a plural noun. God was talking just about one person as the offspring through whom the world would be blessed! Paul writes, "Now the promises were made to Abraham and to his offspring. It does not say, 'And to offsprings,' referring to many, but referring to one . . . who is Christ" (Galatians 3:16).

Abraham was the paradigm of faithfulness. But no human being, not even Abraham himself, could fully live in the fidelity and obedience God required. Now, from eternity the Son has always perfectly loved the Father. In Jesus, the Son stepped out of eternity and into the world, taking up life as a man in flesh and blood. From within our humanity he lived a perfect communion with his Father. He kept the covenant that everyone else had broken through the centuries. In this sense Jesus alone is the true offspring of Abraham, the genuine man of faithfulness.

Since we can't fix ourselves, we need to be joined to Jesus, the only man who stayed right with his Father all his days. We who by nature and practice are disobedient children of wrath (Ephesians 2:3)—we for whom there is something wrong with everything— can never on our own re-enter the blessing of communion with God. We can never independently be children of God or even offspring of the promise to Abraham. But in Christ every possibility opens again. Jesus has kept the law of God's covenant with his people. He has taken the wrath due covenant breakers. He has declared us righteous in him. He has paved the way for us to be adopted into him. The legal possibility of adoption becomes our organic spiritual reality. The Spirit joins us to Jesus. We become the offspring of Abraham in and with Jesus. Men, women, boys and girls can become sons of God and sons of Abraham by participating in the life of the one Son of God.

Paul writes of it this way: "And because you are sons, God has sent the Spirit of his Son into our hearts, crying, 'Abba! Father!' So you are no longer a slave, but a son, and if a son, then an heir through God" (Galatians 4:6-7). Jesus accomplished our sonship in his life, death and resurrection. Now, when we hear and believe, he pours his Spirit into our hearts and so joins us to himself.

All the benefits Jesus won by his faithfulness become ours by faith in him.

Paul explains how we can receive the blessing of Abraham as we are joined to his one offspring. Through our turning away from any reliance on ourselves and turning to rely solely on Christ, we may be made heirs of all his promises. Those who relate to God as Abraham did are included in Abraham's blessing: "So then, those who are of faith are blessed along with Abraham, the man of faith" (Galatians 3:9).

Here is an ancient prophecy of Isaiah gloriously fulfilled: "I will pour my Spirit upon your offspring, and my blessing on your descendants" (Isaiah 44:3). We know from the way Hebrew poetry works that in this verse the gift of God's Spirit is the very definition of the blessing. The passage goes on to say that because of the blessing of the Spirit, future offspring will boldly, faithfully declare, "I am the LORD's." And now we know why: because the Spirit joins us to Jesus. The blessing of God is to unite us to the blessing in the flesh, Jesus Christ, the one true and faithful offspring of Abraham, the promise keeper. Jesus brings us back into communion with the Father and all his blessing love.

In one of his first sermons after Jesus' resurrection, Peter linked the coming of Christ to the fulfillment of the promise to Abraham. He urged his audience to turn to Jesus:

> You are the sons of the prophets and of the covenant that God made with your fathers, saying to Abraham, "And in your offspring shall all the families of the world be blessed." God, having raised up his servant [Jesus], sent him to you first, to bless you by turning every one of you from your wickedness. (Acts 3:25-26)

Peter offers a wonderful nuance in equating the ability to turn to Jesus with a gift, a blessing, from God. Enabling us to turn from trying to work it out on our own (the essence of our sin) to trusting the risen Jesus as our salvation is the way God fulfills his promise to Abraham to bless the world. It's a gift to be able to repent and turn to Christ. It's also a step we must choose to take.

Taken Back in His Arms

Katy Cosby's life went into upheaval in her mid-teens when her parents divorced. Her parents' preoccupation with their own trauma communicated abandonment to Katy. Her child's heart received the breakup as a personal rejection. And her power as an adolescent gave her ways to act out the anger that arose from hurt. She recalls a perilous journey from feeling cursed to discovering blessing.

> Satan exploited my struggles, and as a result I began going down a dark and dangerous path. I began trying to mask my feelings of emptiness and fear with emotional and physical highs to cover it up. As a result I was completely destroying my life; I was living life on my terms, destroying relationships along the way.
>
> But that didn't work out too well. I dropped out of college and worked a lot of dead-end jobs. At one point I even renounced my faith in Christ, believing he had turned his back on me. But really he was with me all the way. There are specific instances where I realize I shouldn't even be here today, but Christ spared me.
>
> After about five years of this, I finally hit rock bottom. My family cut me off, I lost my job and I was on the verge of being homeless. But Christ had a plan for my life. He laid it on my sister's heart to put me into treatment. I was able to come to him completely hopeless, abandoned, on my knees, just asking him to reveal himself to me. And he did! I felt

complete peace and comfort from him. I was truly able to feel his grace. I mean, for him to come and be there for me after renouncing him, denying him and rejecting him for that long—it was truly amazing.

From then on, Christ was able to help heal those resentments and that anger toward my parents. I felt complete acceptance in him. For a long time I resented my past, feeling I wanted it all to be blotted out. But then it seemed like God said to me, "You went through that for a reason. You came to me utterly hopeless and abandoned, and that's how I want you to come to me every day." So I feel like now it is a blessing that I went through that.

With her parents' breakup, Katy felt like she had been orphaned. She did not belong anywhere, so she went searching for love and life recklessly. But God reminded her that she still had a family; he sent her sister to call her back from the brink. As she cried out to a heavenly Father she was not even sure would listen, Katy heard a great "Welcome home!" Her heavenly Father revealed the mystery of how he had adopted her in Christ as his own.

Katy's sister arranged for her to come work at our church as soon as she got out of treatment. Katy laughs to tell how even though she had come to receive the blessing love of Christ, she didn't want to work with a bunch of Christians! She expected to receive only judgment. But she found love and acceptance instead. She got adopted into our family of faith and discovered a whole church full of spiritual orphans who had been brothered by Jesus just as she had.

The road to growth was not always smooth. But another turning point came when the church invited Katy to be part of a mission team in Egypt. She spent a week working at a sports camp, sharing the love of Christ through serving Arab children. A great leap in her transformation occurred as she stepped into the blessing dynamic. Having received the blessing of Christ's grace, she felt the joy of extending the blessing toward others. Katy is just about to graduate from nursing school. She'll make a great caregiver in a hospital. She is a joyful worshiper and a beloved member of our congregation.

Picked Up By the Father

I've recently discovered a reality about the ancient Roman world that stunned me. It horrified me to think that people in the great classic age could be so cruel. But it has set the news of our adoption in Christ in an entirely new, glorious light. In the Roman world, being the biological father of a child did not necessarily mean one had to acknowledge, raise, shelter and care for the child. In a Roman family, the paterfamilias, or head male, had all authority. He decided whether or not the family would accept a new child.

The custom was that after a baby was born in a Roman household, the midwife would place the child on the floor at the feet of the paterfamilias. He would then make a determination about the child. If he picked the child up in his arms, that child was thereafter a member of the family. If he did not pick the child up, the baby would be set outside the home—even if the infant was his own flesh and blood. Then the child would either die of exposure or be picked up by someone else and likely sold to become a slave. This practice seems unimaginable in its barbarity, yet it continued until the first Christian emperor, Constantine, prohibited the abandoning of children.[1]

This is the culture in which the first Gentile Christians came to know the blessing love of Jesus. No offspring was actually a member of the family until the head of the family adopted him as his own. Biology alone did not create the family. In that sense, every child was adopted. The choice of the father to take up his child from the floor created the family. He would become what was called in Latin the *susceptor*, the one who takes up. The susceptor had to take the child as his own, and then the baby could live as a beloved member of the family.

Think of this in relationship to the words we read in the New Testament about the love of God the Father for those he adopts in Christ. Hear Paul's famous framing of the gospel in light of our need for a susceptor to pick us up from the floor of abandonment and take us into the arms of acceptance:

> For when the fullness of time had come, God sent forth his Son, born of woman, born under the law, to redeem those who were under the law, so that we might receive adoption as sons. And because you are sons, God has sent the Spirit of his Son into our hearts, crying, "Abba! Father!" So you are no longer a slave, but a son, and if a son, then an heir through God. (Galatians 4:4-7)

I know Paul was referring first of all to the Jewish law with its requirements for pleasing God. But Paul was also aware of the realities of the Roman world. The young Christians to whom he was writing had been raised as Gentiles. They lived in a culture where every child's life was precarious. So this passage spoke into the rule of the all-powerful paterfamilias. Christ came to redeem us from under the laws of frail, fickle human love on which no one can depend, not even an infant. The true Father God sent his Son into the world to claim us and adopt us as his own.

When we were lying helpless on the floor, he saw us. When we were crying from breathing the toxic air of this world, he took pity on us. When we were helplessly wallowing about in the blood and water of our birth, crying out for food, for care, he saw us, nodded and reached toward us. When we could have been left to die, when we could have been sold as slaves, the Father said, "Mine!" He took us in his arms and claimed us.

In the Roman world, every mother would have trembled, "Will he take up our child?" Every older sibling would have worried, "Will he let my baby brother live?" In fact, we all know that soul fear. We realize our sin has cut us off from our Father in heaven. We feel abandoned down here on the dark planet. We feel cut off in the depths of our souls from the love we yearn for. The future seems precarious indeed. But Christ has brought peace. So Paul would write to the Romans, "For you did not receive the spirit of slavery to fall back into fear, but you have received the Spirit of adoption as sons, by whom we cry, 'Abba! Father!'" (Romans 8:15). Now when we cry, "Abba! Father!" we know that God does not turn cruelly from our cries. He hears us. He sent his Christ to claim us, and he sent his own Spirit into our hearts to bond with us.

In the second century, Irenaeus described this claiming, saving love as the reaching down of the Father's "two hands." The Father sent his Son as his mighty hand to rework the clay of humanity he had made. Jesus remolded the essence of man as he lived a life of communion and faithful obedience. Then the Father sent his Spirit as his second mighty hand to pick us up and join us to this new man Christ and all he had done. I visualize these two great hands stretching out to lay hold of a lost, crying toddler heading for the road. As the saving work of the Son and the faith-creating work of the Spirit come together around us, the Father says, "Gotcha, little one! Come on home now. You're mine and I won't let anyone take you from me." With his two hands the Father picks us up. He calms every fear: "I will not put you outside to die abandoned. I laid down my life for you in Christ so that I can take you up into my love. You will be in my family always."

I remember when our first son, Micah, was little; he was a very compliant child. In the mornings he would play by himself in his crib for quite a while. Then he would call out, "Wake me up!" Obviously he was already awake. In fact, given his agility at an early age, I'm quite sure that if he was old enough to talk, he could have climbed out of the crib. But he wanted the claiming of his parents to bring him into the new day. So I'd go into his room and see him standing in his crib. In his little footed pajamas, he would start to dance. Then he'd hold out his arms with a huge smile and say, "Pick me up!" Could I possibly look at that cute boy and say, "No, not today. You just stay there." The spirit of fathership surged through me. I'd scoop him up and say, "Good morning, busto! Let's go get breakfast." What a privilege, what a joy that for those precious few years I could claim each child as my own every single day.

John writes, "See what kind of love the Father has given to us, that we should be called children of God; and so we are" (1 John 3:1). The Father of all, the one true sovereign, is our susceptor, the one who takes us up. The Father loves his children. He sees our outstretched arms and hears our cry of "Abba! Father!" for his Spirit within us is calling out to him. *Pick me up*, we pray. And he delights to take us in his arms and claim us again and again as his own. Every moment, every second, he is your susceptor. He takes you up as his own, as his beloved, as his heir. What love indeed that we should be called children of God!

John goes on, "Beloved, we are God's children now, and what we will be has not yet appeared; but we know that when he appears we shall be like him, because we shall see him as he is" (1 John 3:2-3). This is who we are now. And more—much more—is coming.

His Name Engraved on Our Hearts

An adopted child receives the name of the family. Sharing in that name signifies that he is truly one of them. At the end of Matthew's Gospel, Jesus sends his disciples into the world to make more disciples. His words can be translated as "baptizing them into the name of the Father and of the Son and of the Holy Spirit" (Matthew

28:19). They don't only go forth in his name; they go to bring others into the name of God.

Now, our adopting heavenly Father has offered his name to his people from the beginning. And this placing of God's name can be a powerful part of weekly worship. The service at our church concludes like this: I say, "If you will receive the name of the LORD your God upon your heart and your life, please stand for the blessing."

And they stand!

Then I lift up my hands and open my arms wide. In turn, many in the congregation hold out their hands in a receptive gesture. I smile as I look around at the faces of the worshipers I have grown to love and say with all my heart,

Now the LORD I AM, Yahweh,
The one true God, who is Father, Son and Holy Spirit,

The LORD bless you and keep you;
The LORD make his face to shine upon you,
And be gracious unto you.
The LORD lift up his countenance upon you,
And give you peace, now and always.

I conclude with an invitation: "And let God's people reply . . . "

Then they answer heartily, "Blessed be the LORD I AM, who is Father, Son and Holy Spirit. Amen."

Afterward I often think to myself, "There, it's done! If I die today, I will have done for my beloved congregation the most important thing I can do. I will have offered the match between the triune God and the people he has called as his own." So we read in Numbers that after giving Aaron and his sons the words of the blessing, God said, "So shall they put my name upon the people of Israel, and I will bless them" (Numbers 6:27).

In this blessing God offers his sacred name. His name represents his identity as a God whose very being is love. So God invites us into the eternal family that is Father, Son and Holy Spirit. On any given Sunday, we may scarcely be aware of how amazing is such grace. Yet we know enough to know we want that name. We've got to have it. We can't live without it. We need God more than we need breath. So as the blessing is pronounced, the congregation accepts the offer. They receive the blessing love of the God who adopts his wayward creatures into his own beloved Son and causes them to become his children too.

As the people turn their faces upward, lift their hands and speak the response, they reaffirm their life in God. They say, in effect, "Yes, I will accept God's claim on my life. I will take his name. I will henceforth and forevermore be known as belonging to the LORD God. Yes, I will be joined to him. My deepest identity will be the triune God who has saved me, claimed me, brought me to life out of death and sent me into his world with the news of his gospel. Yes, bless me! Yes, direct me! You are our God and we are your people."

Until we meet again, we go from worship with the echo of these words in our ears and hearts. Until Christ comes again, we go into the world with the promise of his name blessing us in the depths of our being.

God on Bended Knee

To reclaim an overused word, this benediction moment is *awesome*. It is like no other blessing or benediction. The triune God actually consents to let his name, his personal presence, dwell within his people, both in their individual hearts and in their communion as one people in Christ. The Hebrew root of the word we translate as "blessing" is *berech*: the knee. To bless someone, then, is symbolically to bow the knee toward them. I bend my life down toward the one whom I bless. I offer myself in the service of her well-being. I stoop to be sure I have come to where she is. I have turned from my own interests and activities and positioned myself as being totally for the other person.

For God to bless us with his name, then, means that the great king of the universe bows his life toward ours. If we consider all the religions of the world, we realize that such humility is unheard of in a deity. What god bends down to his worshipers? What king kneels before his subjects? Only the God who lays aside all dignity to pursue frail and wanton creatures like us. The triune God of grace simply will not be without us. He bows the knee to write his name on our hearts. He gives us nothing less than himself. Aaron's blessing, then, symbolizes the giving of the entire blessing story of salvation from the heart of God to us.[2]

By this name the worshipers are both bound and blessed, both claimed and set free, both "homed" and sent to the farthest corners of the earth. They are tied to the mighty saving works of the Father through his Son Jesus Christ in the power of the blessed Holy Spirit. All this God is doing to them in that benediction and they are accepting in their reply. For all this they are now accountable.

Knowing that this is what is involved in Aaron's benediction, could anyone ever dare to miss worship again? Knowing how this blessing utterly claims our lives, could anyone dare to come to church again?

If what I'm saying is remotely true, then it's no wonder I am both exhausted and exhilarated by pronouncing such truth over my beloved congregation. We are all in way over our heads. Yet this depth is exactly what makes pursuit of the blessing life so compelling. It propels us to the second stage of the blessing dynamic as we consider how we return the blessing by praising Christ for his beautiful work in our salvation.

PART TWO

Returning Blessing
to God

PRACTICING THE ART
OF BLESSING GOD

⁓

*O*ne of the most frequently asked questions I hear about the blessing life is "How do I bless God?" People often feel that the idea of our blessing God is a bit silly. After all, it's not like there's something we have that God needs. I can't provision the Creator of the universe. I can't tell him something he doesn't already know. It almost feels arrogant to think that somehow I could be a blessing to God. He always picks up the check, so to speak. He's the host, the master, the provider, the blesser—not me.

While that's true, many times in Scripture we are rallied to bless God. In both the Hebrew and the Greek, the same word for our blessing God is used when the Bible talks about God blessing us. God blesses us and we reply with blessing that is of the same order, if obviously not the same magnitude. Psalm 103, for instance, is emphatic:

> Bless the LORD, oh my soul,
>   and all that is within me,
>   bless his holy name.

Bless the LORD, oh my soul,
  and forget not all his benefits. (Psalm 103:1-2)

David calls us to join him in blessing God with all that is within us, with every effort and all our skill. But what exactly does that mean? One of the lovely qualities of the psalms is that many of them are written as a series of pairs. David says something in one line, then he says it again in the next line in different words. This means that the second line or verse clarifies the first. By that principle, we see from these verses in Psalm 103 that blessing God is equivalent to not forgetting his benefits toward us. More positively, blessing God is remembering and extolling all he has done for us. The song goes on:

who forgives all your iniquity,
  who heals all your diseases,
who redeems your life from the pit,
  who crowns you with steadfast love and mercy.
    (Psalm 103:3-4)

David is rousing his soul to bless God by recalling all the mighty acts of God in his life.

As a further example, Psalm 34 begins, "I will bless the LORD at all times." The next line has the same meaning but clarifies the first: "His praise shall continually be in my mouth." So blessing God has to do with praising him. Praise is a form of blessing and it means well-speaking, adoration, worship. In short, we bless God when we praise him. We praise God when we speak well of him. We do that by saying back to God all he has done and shown himself to be. God's redeemed people are enjoined to bless God; we bless God as we praise him.

Still, you may wonder, "Well, for whose benefit is such praise and worship? Does God really need to hear my croaking voice? Does he who hears the angels sing in a heavenly language actually want my paltry words in one of the primitive languages of earth?" It can seem preposterous that our little bit of worship could matter to the Almighty.

Building God's Throne

But let's think about it from a bit of a quirky angle. If you were the king of the universe, on what kind of throne would you sit? As creator of all, you could make your throne out of anything: diamonds, starlight, angel hair. You could make your throne any size, put it anywhere. Your throne could be a nebula or an atom, an electron or a quark. But what does the God who has everything truly prize as so valuable that he would make his throne out of it? What really shows off his glory?

In Psalm 22:3, David prays, "Yet you are holy, enthroned on the praises of Israel." Another translation says that he "inhabits" the praises of Israel. He takes up his residence as ruler in a throne room echoing with our worship. Out of all that exists in the universe, God chose to build his throne out of the blessings of his people.

But how can a throne be built out of worship? We are obviously in the realm of symbolism here, speaking in metaphor of realities more true than words can express. But let's run with the imagery. Imagine that the God who is everywhere and has everything said, "When I make the human heart, I'm going to withdraw enough of myself that the heart will be able to choose freely whether to love me or leave me. On their own, these human creatures could never affect me. They could never touch me or hurt me—unless I give them that power. And I do. I give them the ability to please me or hurt me. I give them the power to increase my glory by their free choice to praise. I give them the ability to do harm and create sadness by turning away. I give them a heart that can choose. And I will bend my efforts to woo them, to love them so they want to love me back, but I will not force them. And when my people do freely bless me because they love me, out of those praises I will build my throne. I will dwell in their worship. I will sit upon their blessing as I rule the universe."

The praises of his people are what the heart of God prizes as more precious than anything. God cherishes the affection of our hearts. As if he had nothing else to do, he bends his skill to try to win our hearts. We who have no power to speak of in this vast universe have been given incredible influence. We can please our heavenly Father as we bless him. Or we can withhold that praise and grieve his eternal Spirit (Ephesians 4:30). Does it matter whether we sing or pray or speak to God of who he is? We may feel insignificant, but God feels otherwise. He yearns for our love; he treasures our affection. The prophet wrote, "He will rejoice over you with gladness. . . . He will exult over you with loud singing" (Zephaniah 3:17). God is passionate for us. He longs to hear us bless him.

Taking Notes for Creation

The value God places on our expression of worship is stunning, but there is even more to it. Of all the creatures on the earth, we alone have been made in his image. It's impossible to say all that it means to be in the image of God. But we know that at the least it involves being aware and being able to speak that awareness. People have with great effort taught the smartest parrots, monkeys and dogs to recognize words. Dolphins and whales seem to communicate through a kind of language. But only humans can compose sentences that speak the meaning of the world. We alone can realize that there is a God and give him praise. The rocks, the oceans, the trees and the animals give glory to God just by being what they are. They are the work of God's hands and so they glorify him. But only people can speak that meaning. Only we can declare that praise. We are called to give voice to creation.

George Herbert, a seventeenth-century Anglican pastor, once did an extended meditation on this idea of speaking creation's praise. He wrote,

> Of all the creatures both in sea and land
> Only to Man you have made known your ways,
> And put the pen alone into his hand,
> And made him Secretary of your praise.[1]

Secretaries of praise. We take notes for all creation and turn them into words, songs, prayers, symphonies of praise. We call out for the rocks. We sing joy for the trees. We give words to the powerful worship of the waves. We speak the meaning of creation before the Creator. We tell our God, "Be glorified in all you have made. The grass waving in the wind is applauding you. Rejoice, Father, at the bird on the wing, for in her flight she praises your freedom. Let your heavenly heart be glad in the running song of the stream, for its waters, like your worship, never cease to sound. Let your depths be praised to the bottom of the ocean's abyss. Let the reach of your love be praised to the most distant star. Let the gentle ways of your Spirit be spoken on a spring breeze. Let your dangerous glory radiate with the blazing summer sun."

In Psalm 96 David acts as the conductor of blessing worship, first for God's people, then for all creation. He begins,

> Oh sing to the LORD a new song;
>   sing to the LORD all the earth!
> Sing to the LORD, bless his name;
>   tell of his salvation from day to day.
> Declare his glory among the nations,
>   his marvelous works among all the peoples!
> For great is the LORD, and greatly to be praised;
>   he is to be feared above all gods. (Psalm 96:1-4)

The LORD is great and deserves great praise. Such blessing is our calling. We credit God for the glory and praise he is due.

The psalm goes on to use a great word: *ascribe*. David cries out, "Ascribe to the LORD the glory due his name" (Psalm 96:8). Scribes take notes; they write out the words others speak. We scribble on a pad when we take down a number or notes during a call. We ascribe to God when we declare in writing, song or word just how good and great is our God. This is a task given to each of us individually and to all of us collectively when we answer the call to gather regularly for worship. We each give expression in our own unique way to the praise of God, whether as a lone voice in private prayer or in harmony with others.

Psalm 96 concludes with David summoning all creation to join the praises of God's people in enthroning their king:

> Let the heavens be glad, and let the earth rejoice;
>   let the sea roar, and all that fills it;
>   let the field exult, and everything in it!
> Then shall all the trees of the forest sing for joy
>   before the LORD, for he comes,
>   for he comes to judge the earth. (Psalm 96:11-13)

We bless the triune God of grace who exists as Father, Son and Holy Spirit as we give voice to the rest of his creation. We fulfill our purpose in our worship as we call all people and creatures to bless God with us. The joy of blessing God overflows from such psalms as we've considered. They seem to be after a veritable party of praise to our God. Secretaries of praise, we are called to use our holy imagination to take note of the blessing of God occurring constantly in all the great pulsing life of the world. And then we give that worship voice.

In other words: say something, write something, play something, bang something, shout something, dance something, draw

something, give something, add up something, design something—
whatever you can do to give glory to the God of all, do it. Of all the
creatures in the universe, you alone uniquely give this blessing to
God. He waits and longs for your blessing. His throne is richer and
more glorious because of our praise.

Turning Thanksgiving into Praise

We walked under the arbor holding hands. An old, magnificent
vine twined in the wooden rafters above us. Coral rock fountains
bubbled nearby. So far, the evening seemed to be going well. But I
wasn't totally sure. She seemed to like being with me, but was there
anything more than that? Then she said, smiling, "You're such a
romantic!" Suddenly, I knew. I kissed her. And I've been kissing her
for ten thousand more nights ever since.

Those words of blessing advanced our intimacy. They threw a
bridge across the distance between friendship and the love that
leads to marriage. Of course, she didn't say those inviting words to
me out of context. I had, after all, invited her out, treated her to the
French restaurant and driven us to the beautiful fountains where
almost no one else ever came. I had offered her the best, most romantic evening I knew how. And Rhonda did much more than
thank me. She praised me. She blessed me because her heart was
responding to my heart. She made my head spin. She still does.

Blessing God advances communion with him. Praising him creates
intimacy. If you want to experience the life of God in your life, you
must (yes, that's a *must*) engage him in worship. Blessing enhances
the romance that entices us to know the triune God more and more
and so receive ever more deeply his blessing promises. Blessing God
generates the energy that makes blessing others possible.

Worship crosses the separation we feel from the God who loves
us as much as he loves himself. Of course, God is the one who laid
down the bridge by which we come to him. He is the one who

came all the way to where we are and opened wide his arms to his prodigal children. God reconciled us to himself, giving his life for us while we were still living as his enemies (Romans 5:10). He set up, at infinite cost to himself, the entire romance of our redemption. He did it in such a way that we have freedom to respond. Our blessing reply truly matters. When we bless the God who is Father, Son and Holy Spirit for who he is, we are getting up, leaving the land of ourselves and walking back across the bridge toward our home, our marital home, in the triune God.

On that wonderful night of my date with Rhonda, if she had simply thanked me for the evening I would have appreciated the kindness. After all, some of my previous dates had gone so badly that not even a smidgen of polite gratitude was forthcoming. And thanksgiving is bedrock to our life with God. It's the least we can offer him, and it's absolutely called for. Romans 1 tells us that the root of human sin was that "they did not honor him as God or give thanks to him" (Romans 1:21). Acknowledging God with thanks as the source is vital to our being human. There will be no joy, no satisfaction without it.

But that night with Rhonda, I wasn't dispensing charity in hopes of getting back a warm feeling of appreciation. I was wooing her! I wanted to offer her the things that bring me pleasure in hopes she would thrill to share those in my company. When she verbally blessed me by naming who I am (in delight, not scorn), the relationship moved to another, more wonderful level. Her thanks was implied as she offered much more. We connected. So, too, blessing God takes us beyond thanks, which we should never cease to offer, into a more intimate relationship.

This is not easy for us. When I teach on blessing God, I find that many people have had no practice at it. A lot of folks when writing their first blessing prayers simply give thanks to God for the good things he has given them. Those are fine prayers to offer and we all need to do more thanking. And blessing can interweave with thanks or even be built on expressing thanks. We see this when Jesus blesses his Father in gratitude for food (Luke 9:16; Matthew 14:19). But thanks alone does not reach the fullness of what it means to bless God. Thanks names things that I have, that are part of my life. Sure, I acknowledge the source, but it's still all about me. Blessing is praise. Blessing extols the excellence of the giver. The Greek word is *eulogeo*, which means "to say a good word." The Latin at the root of our word *benediction* means "good speech." Blessing God is saying back something good about God. This delights him!

So for those of us who are fairly good at gratitude but beginners in blessing, perhaps we could turn thanks into praise. We could start by making our list of thanksgiving. Thank you, God, for life itself, for providing for my needs, for saving me in Christ, for giving me family and friends, for giving my life a purpose. Then, with a bit of biblical reflection, we can turn those thanks into saying good things about God. *Life.* O God, you breathed into Adam and made him a living human being. You are the breath of my life. As the hymn says, "In all life thou livest, in both great and small. To all life, thou givest, thou ruler of all!"[2]

- *Provision.* You pour forth your goodness like the sun pours forth its rays. You never stop giving to your world.

- *Salvation.* You are the shepherd searching for his lost sheep. You are the Father who welcomed the prodigal. You are the God of amazing grace who saved a wretch like me.

- *Family and friends.* You are the Father of all. You live in a relationship of love as Father, Son and Spirit. You give us to love and be loved as part of being your image.

- *Purpose.* You are not only the source but the ending. All things come from you and to you all things return. Your glory is the goal of all I do.

Blessing God means we reflect back to God who he has revealed himself to be. We name before him what he has done and extol him for it. He prizes our turning thanks into blessing praise because it deepens us in relationship to him. Rhonda's praise of my romantic side boosted our relationship far more than a sincere thank-you for dinner. It indicated that she knew something deep about who I am, and knowing me she did not run but wanted to connect further. Blessing advances relationship.

The Engine for the Blessing Life

My fear when I teach on blessing praise is that people won't believe me. Many of us have little experience in blessing God. Our worship muscles are weak. We are stuck with the character of the minister portrayed by Monty Python comedian Michael Palin. All the praise he could muster was, "Oh God you are so big. You are so very big. You are so very, very, very big!" True, but perhaps we're called to a bit more articulation.

The truth is that returning blessing to God is the driving power in the blessing life. Praise is the engine on which the whole dynamic runs. This is the part that changes our lives most dramatically. It's the part we're most likely to skip—just give me the list of practical ways I can bless people and I'll be fine. But blessing God provides the fuel for blessing others. It's also the means of truly receiving how God has blessed us in Christ. We show that we get it when we reflect back praise for God's benefits to us.

A few years ago I had a profound experience in worship. The Friday before that Sunday I met my friend Steve Strickler (the one with whom I wrote the Genesis musical) at his doctor's office. His physician asked me to be with him when the diagnosis of his brain tumor was given. The very next day was a presbytery meeting. Steve and I fought a losing battle for eight hours over the status of another great friend's ministry. It was church politics at its worst.

No one fought harder or more loyally that day than Steve. After the meeting we talked a mile a minute all the way home. Then we talked for hours with our wives about his condition, about the meeting, about everything. I went to bed emotionally spent and woke up exhausted.

The next morning was Sunday. Steve and I sat together during the early service at the church. We stood to sing praises to our God. It wasn't about us or anything we had gone through together. It was all about Jesus. For three worship songs we didn't even look at each other. We just praised. Then I turned toward Steve. His face was a flood tears. So was mine. We grabbed each other and Steve said, with joy through his tears, "That was most necessary!"

Necessary worship. When life gets so real and so difficult we just can't stay away from God's presence. Necessary worship. I see it every week among those who work the hardest in giving Christ's love to others. Those who get spent up in service—whether it's their job, their family or a church ministry—soar in worship because praise fuels them back up. We come to get caught up in this great blessing mystery of Jesus our Savior. He gathers us before his Father's throne where we can rejoice to be his children. This is just what I need to get out of myself. Paradoxically, getting out of myself in worship is just when I find that God makes me feel most like myself again: restored, forgiven, renewed.

As we close this chapter, I invite you to try what we've discussed. Stand up. (Sure, go ahead!) Hold the book in one hand. Lift your free hand. Speak aloud the words from this song by Thomas Chisholm, "Great Is Thy Faithfulness," which has crossed over to be a favorite of all generations of worshipers and styles of worship. Better yet, sing the words as a blessing to God for his blessing. Say back to him what he has done:

Pardon for sin and a peace that endureth,
Thine own dear presence to cheer and to guide,
Strength for today, and bright hope for tomorrow,
Blessings all mine, with ten thousand beside!
Great is thy faithfulness! Great is thy faithfulness!
Morning by morning, new mercies I see.
All I have needed, thy hand hath provided,
Great is thy faithfulness, Lord unto me.[3]

Can you feel how your heart lifts as you speak to your Father his marvelous faithfulness to his children?

Next, I'd like to take you to five scenes from the life of Jesus as represented in great Christian art. In each picture we will see the blessing hands of Christ. Our work will be to ponder the blessing given in each scene. Then we will join our hearts and voices with some amazing words that have been written through the centuries to bless the Lord Jesus for all his blessing hands mean in our lives.

GOD IS WITH YOU

ᥴℐᕋ

*O*ur first image is a modern rendering of an ancient icon. This form of Jesus within the womb of Mary has been similarly depicted in Christian art for more than a millennium. Icons are meant to be symbolic representations of the ways God has made himself known to us. They are not realistic art in the sense of rendering their subject like a photograph. No artist ever thought Jesus was really a little man who sat up and looked out of the womb! Rather, icons render a deeper reality, communicating the spiritual meaning surrounding the moment when the eternal God entered our world.

Our Lady of the Signs

So we see Mary with her arms raised in a gesture of receptivity. She is accepting the incarnation of God within her. She is praising the Father of her child. The womb of Mary is a window onto eternity, depicted by a perfect circle filled with stars in endless blue depths. We see a baby who is truly human. But his mature features indicate that he is also more than ordinary; he is truly God. His hand is raised in the ancient gesture of a trinitarian blessing. Through these symbols, the icon takes us right to the heart of the Christmas story.

In Luke's Gospel the angel Gabriel appears suddenly to the young Mary (Luke 1:28). Gabriel announces that Mary as a virgin will conceive a son without a husband. God the Holy Spirit will take the place of the human father and that her Son "will be great and will be called the Son of the Most High" (Luke 1:32). She is to call him Jesus, a name that means "God saves." Though this news must have been strange and daunting to her, Mary replies in faith, "Let it be to me according to your word" (Luke 1:38). Let's consider some of the building materials this scene can give us for a throne of praise.

You Are with Me

Gabriel's words to Mary evoke for me a line in Psalm 23, a psalm I have loved since my mother taught it to me as a child. This prayer to God as our Shepherd is one of the most familiar and beloved passages of Scripture, sustaining millions across three millennia and seven continents in every season of life. The heart of this psalm appears as it passes through its darkest description, "Yea, though I walk through the valley of the shadow of death, I will fear no evil, for thou art with me" (Psalm 23:4 KJV). The personal presence of our Shepherd sustains us down the most trying paths. He is with us. We are not spared danger but sustained through it with the immediate sense of God's nearness and the hope for a future of everlasting life in his house.

Now as we look at this icon, we see that these words come even closer to us than David could have known when he prayed them. "Thou art with me." In Mary's womb, God came to be with us so closely that he knit himself to our flesh and bone. As we see Jesus raising his preborn hand in blessing, perhaps we can hear him saying something like this: "I have come to be with you by becoming one of you. What you are is beloved to me. I bless your life in the world by entering it. I, the uncontainable God, give myself to be contained in the virgin's womb. I risk the passage through the birth canal to the daylight world. I am your brother. I will engage human life from birth to maturity to death as you do. I simply will not be without you. You shall be my people, for I am now bone of your bone and flesh of your flesh. From your midst I come to bless you."

One Good Friday, my daughter Mary-Emeline and I went to an Episcopal church for a service. We sang "O Sacred Head, Sore Wounded" and we were both taken with a verse we hadn't remembered seeing before:

> My days are few, O fail not
> With thine immortal power,
> To hold me that I quail not
> In death's most fearful hour;
> That I may fight befriended
> And see in my last strife
> To me thine arms extended
> Upon the cross of life.

These words struck me: "That I may fight befriended." There is no escaping the fight. We will all wrestle with the darkness. Everyone must pass through the valley of the shadow of death. Everyone will fight against difficult circumstances, against sin, against the evil one. But if I might fight befriended. If I might face the hour of trial with my soul's shepherd and friend with me. If I might see, even in the battle with death that I must lose, thine arms extended upon the cross of life. Then I can face it. Then I need fear no evil. For thou art with me. The blessing Christ within the womb of

Mary assures me of this friendship: I am with you.

The final words of Psalm 23, "I will dwell in the house of the LORD forever" (Psalm 23:6 KJV), are on the plaque that marks my mother's remains in the quiet garden of a Presbyterian church in Lenoir, North Carolina. And I want to tell you why. Two months before she died my mom had to be admitted to a hospital for a month of care. In sixty-two years of marriage my parents had never been apart more than a few nights. Dad knew this was the beginning of their mortal separation. In the hospital her dementia only worsened. She knew Dad. She knew me. But she didn't know much else. She became harder and harder to reach. One afternoon I went to visit her and quickly ran out of things to say. She had closed her eyes and just lay there while I talked. Finally I said, "Mom, I'm going to say Psalm 23 for you, because I know you love it." Slowly I spoke the words. She made no response. Then I said the last line, "And I will dwell in the house of the LORD forever." Her eyes opened. She smiled at me. For one second, coherence returned. "I want to," she said.

"I want to." Isn't that the heart of it all? Christ gives himself to us: Thou art with me. He promises us eternal life in communion: I will dwell in the house of the LORD forever. For my mother, when everything was stripped away, when she was reduced to next to nothing, she heard God's voice tell her, "I am with you. So you will be with me forever." She received the gift and offered the simplest, most heartfelt blessing, a reply God cherished. Her heart played its final card in the great struggle for coherence in her disease: I want to.

Of the Father's Love Begotten

When we see in the icon the preborn Jesus blessing, we realize that his coming was part of an eternal plan. This is God within the womb. He is fully a human child yet still the same Son of the everlasting Father who with the Holy Spirit purposed this way of re-blessing the world.[1] Almost seventeen centuries ago, a converted pagan grasped the significance of this in a way few ever have.

Aurelius Prudentius was born in 348 in Saragossa, Spain. He was trained in law and the art of rhetoric and soon realized that his skilled tongue could help him get ahead in Roman government. With all his talent Prudentius rose in position, and his bright, restless mind found an outlet in the political debates of the time. For a long while Prudentius lived for the game. He later wrote, "The keen lust for victory / Drove me to many a bitterness and fall."[2] He must have had more victories than defeats, though, for he became ruler of not one but two cities. He served also as a judge and finally received an appointment from the Roman emperor himself to a military position something like that of a governor. Prudentius was a smart, competent, skillful man of words.

But Prudentius writes that he had something of a crisis when his hair turned white and he entered old age, which he defines as—yikes!—fifty. He started to imagine what would happen when he appeared before his God to give an account of his life. He realized that he had quested for all his positions merely to serve himself. He wielded power only for the earthly thrill of it. Prudentius was living for now, for this world, rather than living for God through the means of this world. He suddenly felt empty, as if he had done nothing with his life.

From then on Prudentius directed his talent to expressing the praises of his Savior:

> [Before] I pass, my sinning soul
> Shall doff its folly and shall praise my Lord,
> If not by deeds, at least with humble lips.
> Let each day link itself with grateful hymns
> And every night re-echo songs of God.[3]

Prudentius's great literary talent brought Christianity a voice it had never had before. He wrote with an excellence of skill to match the sophisticated pagan authors. Prudentius raised Christianity's credibility with the educated elite. He matched the best with his writing skill and did it all in service to Christ. His most famous work is a twelve-poem collection called "Hymns for the Christian's Day," in which he offers us songs of praise for each hour of the day. His words have lasted nearly seventeen centuries and still have the ability to give voice to our praise.

His most famous hymn is one many of us sing during advent, "Of the Father's Love Begotten." Prudentius actually wrote twenty-eight stanzas in this hymn blessing Christ. Let's look at just three that relate to our image:

> Of the Father's love begotten, ere the worlds began to be,
> He is Alpha and Omega, he the source, the ending he,
> Of the things that are, that have been, and that evermore
>   shall be.
>
> He is found in human fashion, death and sorrow here to know,
> That the race of Adam's children doomed by law to endless woe,
> May not henceforth die and perish in the dreadful gulf below.
>
> O that birth forever blessed, when the Virgin, full of grace,
> By the Holy Ghost conceiving, bore the Savior of our race,
> And the babe, the world's Redeemer, first revealed his sacred
>   face.[4]

Prudentius reminds us that the universe came to be as part of the eternal love story of the Father and the Son. Before the worlds began to be, the Father loved his Son and the Son loved the Father. In a mystery beyond description, this love occurred in the "bonds" of the Holy Spirit. The third person of the Trinity was the personal glue, the love (as Augustine said) that ever flowed within the triune being. Indeed, all things were made out of the overflow of this love between the Father and the Son in the Spirit.

More simply put, the universe came into being out of a great love story. In the virgin's womb, this love touched down in the midst of our darkened, broken world. The incarnate God showed his sacred face in the infant Jesus so that we could now enter this love. He tasted the sorrow of this world so that we might be taken into the joy of the eternal love of the Father and the Son. So Jesus told his disciples that they would "know that I am in my Father, and you in me, and I in you" (John 14:20). This is the blessing in the lifted hand of the unborn Christ.

Let It Be to Me

Mary's response to Gabriel's announcement provides a paradigm for the blessing life. She receives the news in believing faith; she offers herself in service to God's plan; she blesses God for who he is and what he is doing. The posture of her hands in our image could well go with her reply to Gabriel, "Behold, I am the servant of the Lord; let it be to me according to your word" (Luke 1:38). She engages the blessing God has both for her and through her to the world. She says, in essence, "I willingly accept the conception of the Son of God. I want to be part of your plan to bless the world through him."

Soon after, Mary blesses God in the prayer we call the Magnificat. Imagine Mary's exultation in her God who chose her for such a crucial, unique role in our salvation. The words arise from the heart of a young woman to praise her God who is also, in a very real way, both her husband and her own salvation:

> My soul magnifies the Lord,
>   and my spirit rejoices in God my Savior. . . .
> For he who is mighty has done great things for me,
>   and holy is his name. . . .

> He has shown strength with his arm;
>> he has scattered the proud in the thoughts of their hearts. . . .
> He has filled the hungry with good things,
>> and the rich he has sent away empty.
> He has helped his servant Israel,
>> in remembrance of his mercy,
> as he spoke to our fathers,
>> to Abraham and to his offspring forever. (Luke 1:47, 51-55)

This is blessing God at its best. Mary's Magnificat is deeply connected to the prayer of Hannah (1 Samuel 2), another faithful woman who had a marvelous conception. This shows that Mary was building the throne of praise out of scriptural materials just as we are to do. Mary saw both the personal aspect of God's dealings with her and the big picture of what God was up to in the world. She recalled what he had done in the past and extolled his covenant faithfulness even as she in faith praised God for what he promised to do in the future. Paul wrote, "So now faith, hope, and love abide, these three" (1 Corinthians 13:13), and Mary's blessing contains all three.

As the story of Jesus' conception and birth unfolds in Luke, we see an abundance of blessing God. Zechariah's son John was born to become the herald and forerunner of Christ. It's not hard to attach our hearts to the prayer of the elderly father who for years thought he would die childless. He rejoiced over his infant son, praising God:

> Blessed be the Lord God of Israel,
>> for he has visited and redeemed his people,
> and has raised up a horn of salvation for us. (Luke 1·68-69)

And, of course, when Jesus was born, it was not only the shepherds who were "glorifying and praising God for all they had heard and seen" (Luke 2:20). The angel announced "good news of a great joy that will be for all the people. For unto you is born this day in the city of David a Savior, who is Christ the Lord" (Luke 2:10-11). And then,

> Suddenly there was with the angel a multitude of the
> heavenly host praising God and saying,
> "Glory to God in the highest,
> and on earth peace among those with whom he
> is pleased." (Luke 2:11-12)

The incarnation and birth of the Son of God as a true human being unveiled the astonishing genius of the triune God's blessing plan for his world. The truth of the symbolism in our icon image is that Jesus was blessing us from the moment of his conception. We in turn join Prudentius, who rallied our blessing worship:

> Christ, to Thee with God the Father, and, O Holy Ghost, to
> Thee,
> Hymn and chant with high thanksgiving, and unwearied
> praises be:
> Honor, glory, and dominion, and eternal victory.
> Evermore and evermore!

7

BLESSED FROM THE CROSS

❦

ﬁ[A]fter the great fire of London in 1666, Christopher Wren designed a grand new church for the city. St. Paul's Cathedral opened in 1710. Its huge dome, so similar in appearance to that of the United States Congress, has graced the skyline as a witness for Christ ever since. Inside, in the central nave under that dome, are four oval "quarter-domes." Since around 1900, each has been filled with a mosaic rendering of a scene from the life of Christ.

The Tree of Life, detail

Designed by William Blake Richmond, our image for this chapter comes from the central section of one of these quarter-domes. We notice immediately the bright colors and swirling branches all around the cross. When we look closely, we see that this glorious vine is growing from the cross itself. Indeed, Richmond depicts the cross of Christ as the tree of life, spreading its branches of grace and forgiveness out across the world. Even the rivers of paradise flow from the base of the cross.

As I look at this image I am reminded of Jesus' words, "Behold, I am making all things new" (Revelation 21:5). Jesus turned the killing cross into the tree of life. Crucified at Golgotha, the place of the skull, Jesus turned the wasteland into the Garden of Eden restored. When something was wrong with everything, Jesus turned all that death into life. The foulest, most broken garbage heap became the flowering vine of new life in him.

Now if we look closely at the hands of Jesus on the cross, we notice something wonderful. Jesus is making the ancient sign of blessing. Rather than being completely stretched out on the beams, his arms are in the position of the raised hands of Aaron's blessing. What's more, the thumb and first two forefingers of his right hand are extended. This is the ancient sign of Christian blessing in the name of the Father, Son and Holy Spirit. Richmond wishes us to see that even from the cross, Christ was blessing us. When we nailed him to the wood beams, Jesus yet extended his love to us.

Father, Forgive

We can plumb the meaning of this image by recalling some of Jesus' words from the cross. When they nailed him to the wood and put him in place to die, Jesus looked out on his tormentors and said, "Father, forgive them, for they know not what they do" (Luke 23:34). The people stood by cursing him. Jesus blessed them from the cross. The people had demanded his condemnation. From the cross he prayed mercy for them. We judged him for death; he prayed for clemency for us. His arms were outstretched in agony. His hands were pierced with nails and pulsing with searing pain. Yet by his words of grace, he turned the pose of execution into the pose of everlasting blessing. Father, forgive them.

Jesus still blesses us from the cross. He speaks truth and mercy to our sin: "The worst that you have done in this world, you have done to me. The sins you committed against my little ones, you did to me. When you neglected the suffering of others, caught up in your own selfish pursuits, you were overlooking me. Your betrayals, your lies, your greed, your failures to act, your scorn, your doubts—all, all of them were against me. You nailed me to this tree. And I, I took your just deserts. I took the punishment due your sins against me as God. And I suffered them as a man on the cross. I paid all the way unto forsakenness by my Father when I was made sin for you. From the cross where you put me, I blessed you. Father, forgive them."

Today You Will Be with Me

Jesus was crucified between two thieves. One railed at Jesus and mocked him. The other cried out in desperate faith, "Jesus, remember me when you come into your kingdom." Jesus said to him, "Truly, I say to you, today you will be with me in Paradise" (Luke 23:43). In the midst of his agony, the Lord Jesus turned to another suffering man and gave him the assurance of everlasting life. He blessed him with the promise of being with him through death into Paradise in everlasting, loving communion.

In the agony that comes to every life in this world, we will each cry out in one of two voices. Some of us will cry out in mockery of God and his love. We will know only bitterness. We will hate God for our suffering and scorn him for not yet delivering the world from its suffering. We will die proud, venomous and alone. But others in our suffering will cry out, like the thief, "Lord, remember me!" We might not ever be able to name the reasons why we have had to pass through such valleys. We might not grasp the redemptive purpose for years, if ever in this life. We may well get angry with God at some points. But we will over time cry out in trust, not accusation.

And so we will discover that God still speaks to us. He speaks not from a life of ease, far removed from our suffering. He speaks from the cross, the same place of agony where we live. He speaks as one who joins our suffering wherever we are. He blesses us as he says, "I am with you now in your suffering. Take courage. Soon you will be with me in Paradise." So we realize that from the cross Jesus enacts the words of Aaron's benediction. Lifted on the rough beams, Jesus is yet God shining on us in favor. Even when we killed him, Jesus was gracious to us. Lined with pain, cut and bleeding, his countenance yet radiated love. The most shameful thing human beings have ever done, putting the incarnate Son of God to death, has become the greatest sign of his blessing grace.

God on a Stick

One year right after Easter, my daughter Mary-Emeline and I traveled to Edinburgh, Scotland. As we walked to the end of the Princes Street Gardens in the center of the city, we came to St. Cuthbert's Church. Noticing that the church was hosting a time of reflection called "Sanctuary in the City," we went in. Various stations were set up around the beautiful sanctuary. At each you could interact with the meaning of Christ's passion and resurrection through prayer, visual art, writing or reading. At one station, I read this poem by Paul Hobbs. Deeply moved, I felt that I had been brought to the heart of Christ's blessing us from his cross.

> They spit on his face and then they crucify him
> Jesus our Lord
> He dies as a sinner
> He dies as a blasphemer, as an idolater, as one who denies God
> As one who betrays him
>
> I stand before the cross and wonder
> He is not guilty of these things but takes our place

He dies as one who boasts, who gossips
As one who dishonors his parents
As a cheat, as a liar, as a thief
He dies as a fraud and an embezzler

I stand before the cross and fear
He is not guilty of these things but takes our place

He dies as a sinner
He dies as one with evil thoughts
As a slave to lust, as a fornicator
As an adulterer, as an abuser of children

I kneel before the cross and weep
He is not guilty of these things but takes our place

He dies as one full of jealousy
As one who is selfish, unkind and rude
As one who destructively manipulates others

As one who envies and hates
He dies as a sadist
As one who destroys and murders

I pray before the cross and rejoice
He is not guilty of these things but takes our place
He is not to blame but dies to take the blame for us

He is dying to forgive us

Stand, stand . . .
And watch Jesus die
Alone and with nothing . . .
God on a stick.[1]

To put together Richmond's mosaic and Hobbs's provocative poem, we might envision once more the hand of Christ raised toward us on the cross. Consider that the pose of blessing is also one of authority. At the moment human power thought it had mastered the Word made flesh, he was yet ruling all things after the counsel of his will. Jesus raised his hand to order the exchange. "He is not guilty of these things but takes our place." He draws us to himself. He takes the worst—the unspeakable, unthinkable worst—and declares with the blessing hand of rulership, "Mine!" With the same nail-pierced hand that even on the cross turned the planets, he declares with all authority in heaven and earth, "Yours! I am yours. Behold, I am with you always, to the end of the age" (Matthew 28:20). So we bless the triune God for the miracle: the hand fastened cruelly to the beam is blessing us.

Amidst Tears Unstoppable Came Joy Unquenchable

Not long ago Rhonda and I experienced the profound depths of being blessed from the cross. At the end of January I was in charge of the retreat for the pastors in our presbytery. I had invited Dr. Wynn Kenyon to be our speaker. Wynn had for decades been a professor of philosophy at Belhaven University. A brilliant guy and a great defender of the Christian faith, he was also an old family friend. As I prepared my introduction, I realized that whenever my life had gotten really hard, Wynn was somehow there. During the most serious challenge to my ministry his wisdom and encouragement proved invaluable. I teared up when I introduced him.

As providence would have it, ten days after he brilliantly led our retreat, Wynn Kenyon experienced a massive heart attack and died a few days later. We could hardly believe it. He was just sixty-four, full of vigor and humor and passion and joy. It seemed like he had a lot more to do in this world. We weren't the only people who loved him. There were two three-hour visitations scheduled, one at the college and one at the church. People poured nonstop through the lines. Wynn had touched many lives. The next day the service was held in the largest auditorium at Belhaven. The sanctuary at his church couldn't possibly hold everyone.

Before the funeral we spent time with the family, trying to be encouraging, then took our seats and waited. A strong desire rose in me. I wanted that service. I craved the hymns and the Scripture. I required someone to speak the meaning of death and resurrection life. It was like waiting for each course of a magnificent meal. At last it began. Though I vocalized nothing, inside my head was a running commentary: *Look, there's the family coming in. Hold close to each other. See how we're all here for you. There's his wife smiling. She won't give in. Look, she's keeping all her chicks together. What a rock! Oh, now here comes the prelude on Psalm 91. Wynn's niece wrote it. Another niece will sing. Can she possibly keep it together?* Yes, just listen: "He who dwells in the secret place of the Most High shall abide in the shadow of the almighty one, the great I Am!" *Yes! Tell me that. Sing me the words:* "My God, in him I will trust."

Then came the call to worship from Psalm 61. I silently called to the worship leader: *Just get the words out, that's all you have to do, the psalm will do the rest.* He spoke, "From the ends of the earth I call to you when my heart is faint. Lead me to the rock that is higher than I." *Glorious! We're at the ends of the earth here in the place of this loss. Get me up on the rock, please!*

Then we stood to sing "In Christ Alone." The congregation sang out. We all needed desperately to declare, "No guilt in life, no fear in death, this is the power of Christ in me. From life's first cry to final breath, Jesus commands my destiny." I couldn't stop crying; I couldn't stop rejoicing. I wanted to bang on the chairs. And still it got better. *Look! The Scripture is 1 Corinthians 15! Oh, buddy, just read the words to me. And if you can mean them as you speak, that will be even better.* "Behold, I tell you a mystery. We shall not all sleep. But we shall all be raised!"

The web of emotions in me was complex. This is the depth of Christian realism. The killing cross can be the tree of life. There can be at the same time grief and triumph, love unquenchable and tears unstoppable. We laughed with the mirth of heaven at the stories they told about Wynn. We squeezed our hands hard as we looked at his family and thought of the days ahead. But through all, in all, above all in that worship there was joy. Looking straight at the reality of death. Looking straight in the face of the pompous power that can reach in and steal a good man from his family too soon, by God's grace we did not crumble or cower. We rejoiced. Because Christ triumphed.

Christ is risen, never to die again. Sometimes we have to get on the cross with him and face the void. But as we bless God, we can see that even Golgotha will bloom. The hand nailed to the cross in agony nevertheless makes the sign of blessing. When evil does its worst, our God gives us his best. At the deepest levels of reality, all is well. Truly well!

8

TAKING OUR HAND
IN THE DARK

⤸

𝒰nderneath the present medieval sanctuary of the Basilica of San Clemente in Rome, an even older church was discovered. You can go down into the ruins and see some of the frescos from the ninth century that have, amazingly, been preserved. One is a painting depicting Christ's descent into Hades. In Christian art, the icons of this episode often depict a similar scene. Jesus appears out of the realm of glory, portrayed by a dark oval behind him that is dotted with stars. His robe is bright in color, representing triumphant glory. The gates of hell lie shattered beneath his feet. Jesus reaches out toward an old man. He helps the man to

Christ's Descent into Hell

rise. That man is Adam. Often, Eve is depicting holding onto
Adam's arm, rising next to him. Sometimes there is a whole crowd
of people behind them, representing all the believers from Old
Testament times. The basic idea is that after his crucifixion, before
Easter morning, Jesus went to the realm of the dead to free the
faithful who had been chained in darkness for millennia.

In the extract from the San Clemente fresco above, you can see
Jesus' hand grasping the wrist of Adam. Adam, the first man,
brought death into the world through his sin. Jesus, the new
Adam, destroys death and opens the way to everlasting life. Christ
stretches forth a blessing hand to Adam, who has been languishing
in the shadows of the netherworld all this time. Adam's hand hangs
limp, for he has no power to clasp back or to free himself. Jesus
alone undoes the ancient curse. He offers a share of his life to the
original image-bearers.

The second image shows what's going on beneath Jesus' feet. As
in so many depictions of the descent, the devil is on the ground.
You can see his small, dark head turned toward Christ. In this
fresco, the devil still has hold of Adam's foot. He wants to keep possession of captive humanity. Jesus, however, has his own foot on
Satan's back.

Remarkably, when I stood in front of this fresco, there was no
one else around. The lower basilica was dimly lit. As I stood in the
damp darkness underground, it didn't take much imagination to
feel as if I too were in the inferna, the realm underneath. I stared at
the painting for a long time. As I gazed, I felt my own life taken up:
I am in Adam. A captive to sin. To selfishness. To self-destructive
behavior. To failure to love. I want to be free. I want to love Jesus
and live in his light. But Satan has hold of me. He wants to keep me.
Satan has Adam by the foot. Jesus has his foot on Satan's back.
What will happen? Who will win that struggle? A thrill shot
through me. Jesus has won that fight already! I could hear his voice

calling to Adam, calling to me, "Get up! Get up! Get up! Rise, Adam. Rise, Eve. Come out of the prison. Come out of the land of death. Be free! Come into life. The gates are shattered. The evil one is crushed. I'm going back up. Come with me! Let's go."

Other tourists came. I could sense them behind me but I couldn't take my eyes off this scene. They didn't stay long. I'm sure they wondered what in this faded image so transfixed me. For several more minutes I couldn't leave. This image spoke to the heart of my humanity with the news of the gospel. The victorious Christ extends the hand of renewed blessing to Adam. The one who once lost it all for all of us would see the deep blessing returned. This news is world-reaching. The possibility for joyful communion with God has been restored—for Adam the man and for Adam's race.

So Paul would write, in a magnificent passage from 2 Corinthians, "In Christ God was reconciling the world to himself, not counting their trespasses against them" (2 Corinthians 5:19). In Jesus God has made his peace with humanity. The gates of death and hell are shattered. Jesus came to the realm of the dead as victor over sin, death and the devil, and now the gospel can be proclaimed throughout the human race. Adam and Eve here represent all of us. The hand reaches forth. The summons is issued: "You may come forth." We rise through faith as his hand grasps us. We let his blessing hand lift us as we trust him. Paul goes on, "We implore you on behalf of Christ, be reconciled to God" (2 Corinthians 5:20). Walk out of death into life as you trust Jesus whose blessing hand laid hold of you.

This is the spiritual truth contained in the phrase from the Apostles' Creed: "He descended into hell." He has come to get us out of prison and out of the tombs. There is no place he would not go to retrieve us. David prayed, "If I make my bed in Sheol, you are there" (Psalm 139:8). Indeed, even when we are hell-bent on running from God and create all manner of hell for ourselves and our loved ones, Jesus goes to the depths with us. He can get us out and bring us home. Even when others open up a can of living hell all over us, when they release the hounds of their madness into our lives, when they empty their evil onto us, Jesus is not daunted nor defeated. He has been to hell and he reigns even there.

I can't say exactly what in this fresco is literal and what is metaphorical. I know Jesus experienced the hell of God-forsakenness on the cross. I know that the descent into hell means Jesus truly entered the realm of the dead. This is a real episode in Jesus history. And I believe he went there as victor, not as victim. The rest is shrouded in mystery. But I can feel in my bones the truth of this image.

And I've seen it work in people's lives.

Defying the Shredder

Recently I met with the elders of a nearby church. Their congregation had applied to enter our denomination, and I was part of a team sent to examine their faith and views. The most moving part was hearing these elders share their testimonies of personal faith in Jesus Christ. I was struck by how many of them had been shredded and devoured in life. One woman told of losing both parents when she was nine years old. Through that she experienced God as her rock from an early age. Years later she passed through a battle with breast cancer and discovered the peace that came to her from total surrender. Now she was caring for a husband who was direly ill. She had been shredded and devoured numerous times, but her joy in Christ was contagious.

Another man told of his hunger for Christ. He had been wildly successful in his business and become confused over what really matters in life. But then that business crashed and burned. He was shredded financially. But the failure moved him to turn back to God. Infinitely more than in his success he found his deep hunger satisfied in Christ. Over time he saw God provide for him as he began to live with a new set of priorities.

Another woman mentioned that Christmas reminded her of an anniversary. One previous December 21 when she was thirty-nine years of age, with two young boys, she watched her husband walk out of the house. She soon discovered that he had taken all their assets and left three months' worth of unpaid bills. But God sustained her. She sought his presence. And God brought her back to life. She is remarried and passionately involved in sharing God's Word with children.

The night before his crucifixion, Jesus said to Simon Peter, "Simon, Simon, behold, Satan demanded to have you, that he might sift you like wheat, but I have prayed for you that your faith may not fail" (Luke 22:31-32). We get shredded. We get eaten up. We get disgraced. We get left. We think we are going to die. But then something amazing happens. We cry out to Jesus and then realize he has already been praying for us! His faithfulness upholds us. Psalm 118 gives us words for this. In utter amazement we realize,

I was pushed hard so that I was falling,
    but the LORD helped me.
The LORD is my strength and my song;
    he has become my salvation. . . .

I shall not die, but I shall live,
    and recount the deeds of the LORD. (Psalm 118:13-14, 17)

We speak right into the teeth of the shredder, "You tried to sift me to bits, but I still live. Now you have no power over me."

Jesus' triumphant descent into hell still gets worked out in our lives. I imagine a puzzled Adam wondering what the God of life was doing down there. How did he survive the death Adam's sin had invited into the world? Jesus in raising him could well have sung from Psalm 118, "I shall not die but live! The world and the evil one did their worst. Now I can't be touched. I will live and recount the deeds of my Father who gave me back the life evil took away." Imagining such a scene makes me want to sing with words that have been on the lips of Christ's redeemed for thirteen centuries:

Thou, grieving at the bitter cry
of all creation doomed to die,
didst come to save a ruined race
with healing gifts of heavenly grace.[1]

Riding the Crazy Train

The mystic experience in the ancient basilica has come to my aid many times, but I especially recall a week one summer when the burden of hell's oppression fell on me. First, tears filled my eyes as a friend spoke about the sufferings of his daughter. "It's like we're riding the crazy train in our house," he told me. "We're trapped in an Ozzie Osbourne song and going off the rails."

My own father's heart broke to hear him, and these words ran through my head: "Jesus suffered under Pontius Pilate. He was crucified, dead and buried. He descended into hell."

The week went on and the stories of evil's triumph kept coming: another shattered marriage; another hopeless financial situation; another wretched, damnable cancer; another journey into grief; pain and still more pain.

The voice of doubt spoke within me. *Boy, what does your religion have to say about all this? It doesn't look to me like God reigns; it looks like death has the last word. It doesn't look to me like a Lord of love is running the show; you all manage to hurt each other pretty well. It doesn't look to me like there's a king on the throne; if your God rules, has he nodded off for a few centuries? It doesn't look to me like anyone is in control except the people who garner a little bit of strength and power for a few years—but they die too. Everyone dies. What've you got to say about that, preacher boy?*

As I wrestled with that voice, I put my hand on the little bronze cross that hangs against my chest. Jesus has been through this. He suffered under Pontius Pilate. He went through hell. That means that somehow my God has accounted for all this. Jesus rode the crazy train. He rode it until it ran right off the rails into a cross and down to hell.

Another voice spoke inside me. *He is here.* I visualized each horrible situation. *He is here. He is here.* I felt the cross under my shirt again. It was old, centuries old. Others—many others, perhaps—had worn it. I had not seen them. I did not know who they were in this world, but I knew who they were in Christ. Others dead and gone—those who lived in times even worse than this—had touched this cross and said our creed. They had spoken the gospel into the teeth of Pontius Pilate and every little tyrant who tried to rule over his own patch of hell on earth.

The accuser, however, kept after me. Pilate's words to Jesus rose in my mind: "Do you not know that I have the authority?" (John 19:10). Powers beyond my control age me, sicken me, trample me, discard me. Treasures evaporate; love gets stolen; little ones get crushed. Hell threatens to gobble up everything. *Do you not know that I rule?*

Locked in the dialogue of this inner struggle, I touched the cross one more time. "No," I whispered. "You do not. Jesus said you would have no authority at all unless it had been given to you from above (John 19:11). Jesus is Lord. Not Pilate or Satan or any other name evil goes by."

I drew on the thousands upon thousands who have dared to meet Pilate's gaze as they recited the Apostles' Creed. Jesus is Lord. He was crucified, dead and buried. He descended into hell. And somehow, in the mystery at the core of the universe, he defeated hell. The death that swallowed Jesus has itself been swallowed by life. I returned to the work of the day with a sense of hope that would not die.

Tom Torrance describes this mystery: "God refused to be alone or without us but insisted on penetrating into the heart of our sin and violence and unappeasable agony in order to take it all upon himself and to save us."[2] He made our death—even our hell—his own. Our fourth-century brother Prudentius voices our praise for this episode in Jesus' story:

> Christ, our Captain, for a season deigned to dwell in Death's
>   domain,
> That the dead, long time imprisoned, might return to life again,
> Breaking by His great example ancient sins' enthralling chain.[3]

The chains are loosed, the dungeon doors are opened. "Get up!" he calls. "Come into life." No power of hell, no scheme of man can keep us from him if we would answer that call. Here is good news beyond hope: the doors of the prison cells of our sin and futility and hopelessness are not locked! We don't have to stay in them. Jesus has conquered death and hell. We don't have to stay there. We don't have to go there. We can bless the Son of God who went to the place of utter forsakenness so that we might live in eternal communion with him.

9

RAISED TO BLESS GOD

⁓

We journey now up from Rome to the city of Sienna in Italy. Let us go to the great cathedral at the heart of this town in the Tuscany region. Inside the buildings of this ancient church, you will find a painting by the Tuscan artist Duccio. Dating from around 1310, it is titled *Christ Appears Behind Locked Doors*.

We read in John 20 that on the evening of the first Easter, the disciples were gathered in the upper room. The doors were locked for they feared they might also be arrested. But suddenly Jesus came and stood among them. He spoke, "Peace be with you" (John 20:19). Notice in Duccio's painting how the disciples are staring at Jesus in wonder and devotion. And see how his right hand is raised—in the gesture of blessing!

The Apparition of the Apostles and the Closed Door

The Gospel tells us that Jesus then showed his disciples his wounded hands and pierced side. The crucified Jesus who was alive again in the same body truly stood among them. He spoke again, "Peace be with you."

As they thought about it later, surely the disciples recalled what Jesus had said to them just a few days earlier. "A little while, and you will see me no longer. . . . You will be sorrowful, but your sorrow will turn to joy. . . . I will see you again, and your hearts will rejoice, and no one will take your joy from you" (John 16:16, 20, 22). The joy that is the goal of the blessing life is anchored in the resurrection of Jesus. It is as sure as his triumph. Blessing takes us into relationship with Jesus and so releases that joy.

The disciples did not understand what he meant at the time. But Jesus wanted to sear the words into their heads for later. So he concluded, "I have said these things to you, that in me you may have peace. In the world you will have tribulation. But take heart; I have overcome the world" (John 16:33). Not only joy but peace is his gift to us. With the resurrection, it all made sense. Peace be with you. Jesus is here. He has overcome death. He has overcome the evil in the world. Peace.

Just as Jesus still speaks blessing from the cross, so he still speaks the blessing word of resurrection peace to us. We have noted that the blessing life does not guarantee any measure of success, prosperity or health. There is no promise of smooth sailing in our daily lives. In fact, we are promised just the opposite: "In the world you will have tribulation." For the children of the covenant who have been joined to Jesus, it's tough out there. You're going to get hurt. Things will fall apart. Great plans will come to nothing. Just when you think you have seen it all, people will shock you with their actions. You will be left; you will be scorned; you will know pain, insecurity, confusion and hardship. But Jesus tells us to take heart. I love the wording of the King

James Version here: "But be of good cheer." Cheer up. Even in tribulation. Christ has overcome the world.

The gospel news is of an all-or-nothing venture undertaken by our blessing God. He pursued us all the way into the far country of our lost and forsaken condition. He ran his game plan until it killed him. The final report is simple and all encompassing: Jesus is risen. Therefore life wins. Death loses. God wins. Satan loses. Grace wins. Sin loses. Jesus is risen and he comes to us even now within locked doors saying, "Peace be with you."

Let's consider how the news of this story rallies us to bless the triune God even today. We, too, may well have locked the doors against the world. Hurt in love, many of us have locked the doors of our heart, hoping never to be vulnerable again. Betrayed, we have locked the doors of hope and put on a mask of clever cynicism. We don't ever again want to be surprised and embarrassed for trusting. We will be negative first; we will expect the worst and mock anyone trying to love in good faith. Struck down by failures, we have locked the doors against the world, hiding away the passion that used to urge us to dare more, try more. We will not venture out again. We will not show what matters most to us to anyone.

But the risen Jesus trampled the gates of death and hell. He is not kept out by any paltry locked doors. They don't stop him. He comes to us with a blessing hand upraised. "Peace be with you." He shows us his wounds. "Look, I understand. I bear the same wounds you have. I was pierced for my faithfulness, mocked for my trust, cursed for living out my passion to bless. I died at the hands of those I came to save. But I live again. I have overcome the world. See my wounds. See how I have been where you have been. See me alive again. You too will live again. Not only in the next life but in this life! Be of good cheer."

But there is more. Jesus had work for his followers to do. John's

Gospel tells us that Jesus went on to speak peace to them a second time, adding a mission for his disciples: "As the Father has sent me, even so I am sending you" (John 20:21). Then he breathed on them the Holy Spirit. They were not going to be allowed to stay in seclusion. Hiding away was not an option. This moment speaks strongly to us when we have been living behind locked doors. Jesus tells us that having been hurt doesn't put us out of the game. Being afraid doesn't get us out of his blessing mission to the world. Jesus still speaks to each heart, "I died and now I live. I was sent to love and you are sent to love. You are sent to bear witness to the fact that I conquered death. Get out there. Betrayal, hurt, death do not have the last word. I am alive. Peace be with you. Be of good cheer. Take heart even as you go forth into a turbulent world."

Again we have a link to Aaron's blessing. That all-important indicator of God's blessing heart concludes, "The LORD lift up his countenance upon you and give you peace" (Numbers 6:26). Jesus spoke the graciousness of forgiveness from the cross. He spoke the peace that passes understanding in the upper room on Easter Day.

Seeing the Wounds

Our second image of the resurrected Jesus depicts a scene described in John 20. Thomas had not been with the others when Jesus first appeared. He simply could not believe the news of the resurrection. It seemed too fantastically good to be true. When the other disciples told him, "We have seen the Lord," Thomas replied, "Unless I see in his hands the mark of the nails, and place my finger into the mark of the nails, and place my hand into his side, I will never believe" (John 20:25).

Eight days after Easter, Jesus once more appeared in a room whose doors were locked. This time Thomas was with them. In this vivid 1603 painting by Caravaggio we see Jesus saying to him,

Incredulity of Saint Thomas by Caravaggio

"Put your finger here, and see my hands; and put out your hand, and place it in my side. Do not disbelieve, but believe" (John 20:27). The man we know as doubting Thomas then made the strongest affirmation of Jesus' identity in all of Scripture: "My Lord and my God!" (John 20:28). Jesus showed Thomas his wounds and it had a transformative effect. It still does.

On that same trip to Scotland I went to visit Mary Torrance, wife of my late beloved theology mentor James Torrance. As we talked that April morning, Easter was still on our minds, along with the trouble in the world and the ache of losing one's beloved. Mary quoted to me from a poem by Edward Shillito written shortly after the bloody horror that was World War I. Shillito, a pastor, had served in that war, and he was among the first to articulate how the illusion of human progress and a war to end all wars had been shattered. Proud modern man was lost. Only the truth of the Jesus of the scars could comfort us. I was delighted when Mary sent me the full text. I hope that through its words you will bless the God who has shown you his scars:

If we have never sought, we seek Thee now;
Thine eyes burn through the dark, our only stars;
We must have sight of thorn-pricks on Thy brow,
We must have Thee, O Jesus of the Scars.

The heavens frighten us; they are too calm;
In all the universe we have no place.
Our wounds are hurting us; where is the balm?
Lord Jesus, by Thy Scars, we claim Thy grace.

If, when the doors are shut, Thou drawest near,
Only reveal those hands, that side of Thine;
We know to-day what wounds are, have no fear,
Show us Thy Scars, we know the countersign.

The other gods were strong; but Thou wast weak;
They rode, but Thou didst stumble to a throne;
But to our wounds only God's wounds can speak,
And not a god has wounds, but Thou alone.[1]

Of all the ideas about God in the world, only the triune God of grace has been revealed as sovereign yet seared with the wounds of his reaching love. Christ's cross is his throne. From it he reigns in kingly grace over both law and sin. But Shillito reminds us that our king stumbled under the weight of that cross on the way to raising it as his throne. If we now would build him a throne of praise that truly uses the materials he has given us in his revelation, then we must erect it with the words "And not a god has wounds, but Thou alone."

Sharing Scars

A young woman from my church traveled to Romania on a mission trip. She joined others from around the world at the Smiles Foundation, a mission agency dedicated to restoring joy to the Romanian orphans through the love and message of the gospel.

During the week, members of the team made home visits for prayer. And the students found that the act of Americans coming from so far away to visit a very humble home was a great encouragement in itself to the people. But even more could be shared across the language and culture divides.

In one home, the woman from my church met a man with deep, angry self-inflicted scars up and down his arms and on his chest. Through a translator he told of the grief of losing his mother at too early an age, of the defeat of not being able to earn enough to feed his family, and the despair that his wife was dying of AIDS. He was wounded at every level. In that house, at that moment, the young woman felt compelled to roll up her sleeves and show this man two things. First she showed him the crisscross of light scars up her forearms from an earlier season of depression. She brought two fingers to her lips. Then she touched her fingers to the man's wounded arm. His tears began to fall. Then she showed him the second mark. It was a small tattoo on her left wrist. She had the translator tell the man the words: "By his wounds I am healed."

He replied by telling her that only God could heal his wounds. For on the literal level, in his despondency, he had not cleaned his wounds and infection could well have killed him. On the spiritual level, he knew he had no personal strength with which to heal his inner wounds. The next day, our young woman sent over to him a stone with the Romanian word for "hope" painted on it. She showed me the picture of his smiling face as he showed the rock to his wife. The communion of scars between the two brought home the truth of the God who still raises the dead and brings hope to the hopeless. "We must have Thee, O Jesus of the Scars."

Two forefingers, just the same two used in the sign of blessing, held up to lips, then touching scars. The blessing hands of the resurrected Jesus still speak, wound to wound, "Peace be with you." My Lord and my God!

10

Blessing Hands Above

cx/o

*W*e journey back across the ocean now as we see the stained glass ascension window from First Presbyterian Church in Baton Rouge. Constructed in 1926, the colorful window shows Christ going up in the cloud of glory. Once again, look closely at his right hand and notice that it is raised in the gesture of Christian blessing.

So we turn to the very end of Luke and read, "Then Jesus led them out as far as Bethany, and lifting up his hands he *blessed* them. While he *blessed* them, he parted from them and was carried up into heaven" (Luke 24:50-51, emphasis added). This scene, then, is not an artist's speculation but a Gospel report. In the world we inhabit, at a particular time, the resurrected Jesus actually did ascend. He went up toward what we know

The Ascension Window

as the sky until the cloud of God's glory removed him to the heavenly realm. He ascended and then entered a dimension to which no vehicle can carry us. From that heaven he will one day come again.

Since the time I wrote a full-length book on Christ's ascension,[1] I have discovered many more treasures on the topic. In fact, the work of two fine theologians, one Reformed and one Roman Catholic, link the ascension to blessing in ways I had never considered. The insights of Covenant College professor Kelly Kapic and Pope Benedict XVI (formerly Joseph Ratzinger) have provided much of the motivation for me to pursue this study of the blessing life. With gratitude to them, I'd like to lay out some of the abundant building materials for the triune God's throne of praise provided by the ascension.

The Reach of Blessing

Luke tells us twice for emphasis that as he ascended, Jesus lifted his hands and blessed the disciples. Think of this scene in terms of perspective. If one Sunday in our church I walked down from the pulpit and stood over one person in the pew, lifting my hand in blessing, all of the congregation might watch, but only the one under the shadow of my hand would feel that the blessing was for him. My hand would be too close to the one person to be for any others. But if I stepped back, I could spread my hands over several pews of people. Then if I returned all the way up to the pulpit, the entire congregation would fall visually under that sign of blessing.

When Jesus ascended upward in the cloud of glory, his blessing hands covered more and more of the land beneath him. His blessing was meant to embrace the world. The news of the gospel was an invitation to everyone to take shelter under those arms. The blessing of Abraham included a promise that "in you all the families of the earth shall be blessed" (Genesis 12:3). Now here was the fulfillment of that blessing. First it narrowed to the person of

Jesus in his ministry on earth, then it began reaching from him round the globe as the benediction was pronounced in his ascension. The ascended Jesus is over us pouring forth his blessing Spirit across the world. Indeed, this is what the prophet Joel predicted: "And in the last days it shall be, God declares, that I will pour out my Spirit on all flesh" (Acts 2:17). His blessing reach is as wide as east is from west.

The Glimpse of Love

This was the last sight the disciples had of Jesus. Those arms, so recently stretched out in agony on the cross, were now stretched out in triumphant love. Jesus' final gesture with us in the flesh was blessing. If you look at a bright scene, then close your eyes, you will notice that the last image you saw lingers on the inside of your eyelids. Visually speaking, the last thing you see is what lingers on in the mind's eye. This picture, then, of hands raised in blessing as the bright cloud of God's glory enveloped him is what Jesus wanted to burn into the disciples' minds. The last words spoken in that unique tenor of voice that belonged to the incarnate Son of God were blessing words. He wanted his benediction to echo in their ears.

The Puritan writer John Flavel spoke tenderly of this scene: "There was a great deal of love manifested by Christ in this very last act of his in this world. The last sight they had of him in this world was a most sweet and encouraging one. They heard nothing from his lips but love, they saw nothing in his face but love, till he . . . was taken out of their sight."[2] Through all they would go through in the coming years, the disciples had this blessed sight for encouragement.

The Parting Gift

At the same time, this departing gesture of Jesus was the prelude to the explosive blessing he would send on them ten days later. On Pentecost Sunday, the room shook as the Holy Spirit descended upon the praying disciples. Tongues of fire danced above their heads. They began to speak of the mighty works of God in languages they previously had not known but that represented the languages of all the pilgrims gathered in Jerusalem. A huge crowd gathered to see what it all meant.

Jesus had promised the gift of the divine Helper following his departure (John 14:25-26). The Spirit would come in power so that they could witness compellingly to the resurrection of Christ throughout the world. Through the Spirit the believers were mystically united to Jesus. He became closer to them by his Spirit within them than he was when he spoke to them in the flesh. As we've often mentioned, the deep meaning of blessing is communion with the triune God and one another. So after the conclusion of Jesus' earthly ministry, we see all three divine persons involved in this blessing. Peter preached, "This Jesus God raised up. . . . Being therefore exalted at the right hand of God, and having received from the Father the promise of the Holy Spirit, he has poured out this you that you yourselves are seeing and hearing" (Acts 2:32-33). Jesus left physically but nonetheless came closer to them through the gift of his Spirit. He departed in blessing but then returned to them in the blessing of his Spirit within and upon them.

Whenever You Look Up

At the beginning of Lent the year of this writing, Pope Benedict XVI released yet another masterwork on the person and work of Christ, this one focusing on the events from Holy Week to the ascension. Though I remain happily a Presbyterian, I drew deep spiritual nourishment and insights from Benedict's book all lenten season. I was especially moved by his final chapter about Jesus' ascension. Benedict writes,

Jesus goes while blessing, and he remains in that gesture of blessing. His hands remained stretched out over this world. The blessing hands of Christ are like a roof that protects us. . . . In faith we know that Jesus holds his hands stretched out in blessing over us. That is the lasting motive of Christian joy.[3]

The blessing hands of Christ are over us. Whenever we look up at the sky, we can imagine the ascending Christ with his arms outstretched. Wherever we go, we go under the sky above us, so wherever we go, we go under the blessing protection and the blessing mission of the Lord Jesus. As Benedict wrote elsewhere of the disciples, "They knew that they were forever blessed and stood under blessing hands wherever they went."[4]

The implications for daily life are stirring. How hard are circumstances pressing you? Can you yet look up and see sky? That sky represents the blessing hands of Jesus keeping you even through these days. Have your powers been curtailed by illness or age? Can you at least still imagine sky? Let it remind you of the one who claims you and loves you. He went up to heaven still in the body. He is still wedded to our humanity. He has promised that he will transform our lowly bodies to be like his glorious body (Philippians 3:21)—we too will live in rippling, embodied resurrection life. How hopeless does the future of the world seem? How far does the arm of evil reach? Look at the sky and remember Jesus' blessing hands. Evil cannot ever go where Christ is and pull him down into our mire. Nor can it ever prevent his return to set all things right. He is still over us like the sky, his blessing hands like a great shell of protection all of our days on this earth.

The True Future of Man

One more lovely insight from Benedict adds to our materials for blessing the God who blessed us in his ascension. We have seen that Jesus is the new Adam. We know from Scripture that Jesus is "the image of the invisible God" (Colossians 1:15). As the man who lived in unbroken love and oneness with the Father, the incarnate Son of God restored the image of God in humanity. This restored image is lifted up before the world as Jesus rises in the sky.

Benedict recalls the words Pilate spoke when he presented the bloodied and abused Jesus to the mob demanding his crucifixion: "Behold the man!" (John 19:5). The Roman governor said more than he knew. This abused figure of a man was reflecting the depraved humanity that flowed from us onto him. Such a corrupted view of humanity is common in our arts and media today as they present "debased man in all stages of horror. That is man, they tell us again and again. . . . To be sure the image of Adam is fallen; it lies in the mud and is muddied over and over again." Left to ourselves this is all we are and all we can be. In hiding from God humanity believes the lie that this is the sum total of our existence. We live in despair.

But, writes Benedict, Christ's ascension says Pilate's gesture is not the whole story. In his ascension Christ has taken our humanity to the right hand of God. "Christ has raised the image of Adam: You are not simply dirt; you extend over all cosmic dimensions up to the heart of God. Christ's Ascension is the rehabilitation of man. . . . It tells us that man can live toward the above . . . that the actual and true place of our existing is God himself and we must ever view man from this vantage point." This is a vision of immense hope. "Behold the man!" on Pilate's lips puts our face on fallen, degraded Adam. But since the ascension, "Behold the man!" shows us a new humanity. Here is the destiny of those joined to Jesus: life renewed, transformed, elevated, outfitted for heaven and taken into communion with God. This is the inner meaning in the sight of Jesus' blessing us. The possibility for humankind to be more than fallen has been opened again in Christ.[5]

The Lord Jesus' Actual Face Shining

Kelly Kapic has argued powerfully for the possibility that Jesus' final blessing was that of the high priest giving Aaron's benediction to the people after atonement for sin had been made. The branding blessing from Numbers 6 takes on even more significance if we consider it coming from mouth of the incarnate Lord himself. Kapic's conclusion thrills me every time I read it:

> Whereas Aaron could lift his arms and pray for God's face to shine on the people, in seeing Jesus ascending into the heavens these believers saw the actual face of God shining. While they had heard of God's graciousness, now they had seen him who is Gracious. While they had held out for God's lifted countenance, they now saw it actualized. While they had longed for the peace promised in the benediction, they now knew him who was Peace. The great High Priest came and not only pronounced the benediction, but he *became the benediction*. Here the medium is the Mediator, and thus he is not to be looked beyond, but rather looked to. Those who saw the ascension *witnessed the personification of Aaron's benediction in Jesus Christ!*[6]

The disciples saw the centuries-old longing of God's people being fulfilled before them. No longer through a priest representing God but by God himself in the flesh were they branded with his name and marked forever as his own. They knew it was a gift of incalculable worth to see Jesus and know him for who he truly is. They knew that to be among those who believed when so many had rejected Christ was truly a miracle akin to the creation of the cosmos out of nothing. So Paul would write years later, "For God, who said, 'Let light shine out of darkness,' has shone in our hearts to give the light of the knowledge of the glory of God in the face of Jesus Christ" (2 Corinthians 4:6).

Luke tells us that the disciples worshiped the ascending Jesus. Then they returned from that event filled with great joy. For the next many days, they "were continually in the temple blessing God" (Luke 24:53). They had entered the blessing loop, receiving and returning. They had joined the massive blessing project of God in the world.

Consider their joy in relation to the images we have explored. How might receiving the same blessings fire us up to join them in the great joy of continually blessing God?

Blessed from the Son of God's conception in Mary's womb, they had heard and seen God in the flesh.

Blessed from the cross, they knew the grace of his forgiveness.

Blessed from his descent into hell, they had taken the hand extended from the new Adam to the old and so been born anew.

Blessed in the upper room, they knew the peace of his resurrection even as they knew themselves sent to the world with the news of the gospel.

Blessed by the ascended Christ, they knew his presence would keep them always, even to the end of the age.

This is the Lord God himself shining on us. For here is Jesus our Lord, God come among us, himself promising to bless us and keep us all the days of our lives.

11

LIVING IN
THE BLESSING LOOP

～

$\mathcal{T}$here is a little valley hidden in the woods I love to hike. Tall poplars, maples and oaks rise to create a great canopy. I feel like I'm walking inside a natural sanctuary. Some saplings rise toward the few gaps in the green dome, their branches extended to catch any light the mature trees haven't blocked. On a clear morning, a sunstream shoots through a gap in the hills and the forest shines. The sun pours forth the rays that make possible the miracle of photosynthesis. The leaves, particularly of the saplings, seem to stretch up toward the sun, offering themselves to the light that makes their life possible.

I feel like I am part of a magnificent worship service. I lift my hands in praise. I extend myself like the branches receiving this glimpse of glory. I give myself back to the Father whom I acknowledge as source of all. The sun and the trees, of course, are not aware of the exchange they are making. This silent drama occurs every clear day and most times there is no person present to imagine any deeper meaning. But when I am there, I feel the privilege of being a man made in God's image. It's a joy to give voice to

what the rest of creation can enact but not say. In prayer, I name
the shining reality that the sun and trees reflect.

God spoke. The world came into being, giving him glory just by
its existence. God sustains creation constantly. He pours forth his
power like the sun its rays. So the universe continues rather than
winking out of existence. When we get this, we worship. We acknowledge that every moment is a gift constantly given. We are
upheld not because we are necessary but because God is faithful.
Realizing this moves us to make our thanks.

We have been given the mind and language to speak back praise.
God makes himself known. We receive his love even as we lift our
hands, hearts and voices to acknowledge him as the abiding source.
But more happens as well. Our praise is connected to the rest of
our lives. What and who we worship shapes our thought of what
the world is all about. When we bless God by telling him back who
he is and what he has done, we are stepping into his story of dealing
with the world. This becomes the narrative that directs our lives.
There is actually nothing more practical than praise. What we bless
becomes what matters to us. What matters creates what we do. So
our offering of worship leads our reply to God's blessing love in our
lives. We receive and make a return that involves giving our whole
selves to God.

This is the blessing loop. It has to do with offering. God creates.
God reveals. God works in us so that we can recognize him. God
offers himself to us. He asks that we give ourselves in return. We
do. We give thanks. We bless him with our praise. We yield our
wills to God's will. We offer him our lives, our very bodies, as a
living sacrifice (Romans 12:1). Then, as we will consider in part
three, we engage in loving service to others as he leads us. We advance his gospel in the world. As we do so, we step into the loop of
love. For whatever we give back to God he goes on to return in
even greater measure. This kind of life is the exact opposite of

being stuck in yourself. This dynamic wheel turns by mutual offering, mutual revealing and mutual sharing between the Creator and his redeemed image bearers.

When we respond by blessing back the God who has blessed us, the triune God responds to our response and blesses us more. Of course, we remember that his blessing is not necessarily getting more earthly stuff. Nor is it having our fondest wishes fulfilled. But we may count on God's always offering the essence of blessing: a deepening communion with himself. So in blessing God and entering the loop, we actually see more of God's activity in our lives. He shows us more of himself in his Word. He offers us a part in his ongoing work of blessing the world. He gives us his energy and power as we do. So overall we become more aware of his presence in us and the world. This causes our hours to be lit up with higher purpose. Increased blessing creates joy. Such exultation runs deeper than any current circumstances. In fact, the experience of joy can be more vivid when life is hard than when our situation seems outwardly "blessed."

The blessing loop is simple: God blesses. We bless God in return. We bless others in obedience. Then God blesses us more. Yet this simple dynamic can carry us through all our years. As we receive and return blessing, the loop starts moving. So we thank God more and worship him more. This in turn opens us to yield more, and so be directed more by God, and so see even more of what he is doing. On it goes, the blessing loop becoming ever more dynamic, catching up our lives in joy as it turns. Now let's consider a wonderful means our Lord Jesus gave us for staying in this blessing loop.

Hoping for Scraps but Given a Feast

The last Sunday before I moved from North Carolina to Baton Rouge, I went to an Episcopal church. Rhonda and Mary-Emeline had already left town. Two of our other children, Jacob and Leah, went back to our Presbyterian church. But all my goodbyes had already been said and I wanted to worship without creating any disturbance. So I went by myself, soaking in the words of the liturgy based on forms the church has used for centuries. When the time came for communion, I went forward to kneel at the rail. I was alone, a pastor between churches, a father between homes, a husband without his wife, a man between times. Layers of pride and self-absorption seemed to have been peeled away by my circumstances and the truth of the ancient words. Kneeling at the rail, I felt myself to be a beggar before the king. I was a supplicant. I had nothing to bring, no scrap of worthiness to offer. I held up my hands with no demands, only the rawest plea.

Just a crumb, I thought. If I could just have a crumb from the table of God, it would be enough. A tiny crumb, a stale crumb, a moldy crumb, just a speck, just a scrap. Oh give me but the smallest morsel and I will be satisfied! Lord Jesus Christ, have mercy on me, a sinner. Just a crumb.

But as the wafer was placed in my hands, with the words, "the body of Christ," the truth of it came crashing through me. I tremble to plead for a crumb. Jesus replies by giving me his entire ascended, glorified body. I do not deserve a speck, but God gives me himself, all of himself. Then the chalice was put to my lips. What, the cup too? For me the beggar? "The blood of Christ poured out for you." This seemed beyond hope. God invited me to drink from the festive cup the wine of the new covenant. To the abject beggar in his rags is offered the chalice of God.

A psalm came to mind: "The LORD is my chosen portion and my cup" (Psalm 16:5). What do you get when you come to the Supper, you compromised, double-hearted, double-minded, befouled cur? The triune God of grace himself is your portion. One drop would be beyond an eternity of deserving, but he pours in the unending wine of his presence. The cup overflows. The cup of salvation.

Christ drank down the dregs of my sin and passed back the chalice filled with his precious blood, the wine of everlasting life.

Eternity crashed in on me. To all appearances it was just an ordinary Sunday. Regular people coming forward to partake of the usual Eucharist. I was merely one of them. It's just that no communion is ordinary. Every time the Word is preached and the Supper is offered faithfully, Jesus gives us himself. His blessed Spirit closes the distance between heaven and earth. We get taken up to Christ and Christ comes down to us. I left exulting in how the Father feeds his children.

God's table is the place where we regularly offer our lives to him and where he promises to give himself to us. This is the usual place where we enter the extraordinary, supernatural blessing loop. All our reasons to bless God are gathered in the communion prayers because they recount his mighty work of creating and redeeming us. These prayers are known in many traditions as the Great Thanksgiving. Christ blesses us by feeding us with his body and blood through the mysterious work of his Holy Spirit. What could be more graphic and graspable than this: Do you want Jesus? Eat him. Drink him. Communion is the gift Jesus gave to his disciples as the continuing way for them to stay in his blessing loop. The Supper represents a way that Jesus asked us to bless him.

Communion is the heart of the blessing life, and so frequent participation in the Eucharist is vital. This is the way God affirms his covenant, "I am your God and you are my people." It is at the Supper that we receive the strength of his commitment to us. His presence encourages us to carry on in joy even amid the inevitable suffering of life. I remember once at a service hearing these words pop into my mind: "The soft snap of the host in the Eucharist is our only answer to the cacophony of the world's tumult." Of course it could just as well have been "The quiet sound of bread tearing" or "The small splash of wine poured into a cup." In the Supper we hear God's still small voice of love amid the noise of life. God's giving of himself to redeem a lost and broken world is our best—indeed only—hope. As we partake we seal the relationship of the God who withholds nothing of himself from us. We eat and drink giving thanks in faith and enter the mystery of love. The sacrament gives us the continuing assurance that Christ Jesus "will sustain you to the end" because "God is faithful, by whom you were called into the fellowship [communion] of his Son, Jesus Christ our Lord" (1 Corinthians 1:8-9).

If you are part of a church that celebrates the Supper regularly, you are in position to enhance your participation through recalling the biblical insights we uncovered here. If your tradition celebrates infrequently, I encourage you to seek out midweek services of communion in other Christian traditions that would welcome you.

PART THREE

REFLECTING GOD'S
BLESSING TO OTHERS

BLESSED TO BE A BLESSING

✎

*M*y friend and colleague Barry Phillips once lived in Charlotte and worked in the telecommunications industry. He was happily settled there with his wife and two daughters. One day, though, a dream job was dangled before him. Promises were made of a lot of money, freedom to manage and unlimited growth potential. It seemed too good to pass up, in spite of the family's contentment in North Carolina.

Barry felt that he and Becky truly consecrated the decision to Christ. They weren't greedy. They knew better than to play the world's game for its own sake. But the future security seemed too great a blessing to ignore. They moved to Little Rock. Barry was miserable. The job was full of stress and he never felt like he got on the same page with the head of the company. What promised to be a great advance turned out to be a weight dragging down the family. They lived less than a year in the new dream house they had built. When a job opened up in his hometown, the family moved to Baton Rouge.

Barry and Becky reflected for years on why they had felt so confirmed to go to a city and a job that turned out to be such a wrong fit. Had they really just totally missed God's will? Then Barry finally realized what had happened in Little Rock. In that brief time, his younger daughter Molly discovered her gift and her calling. A learning disability had made her wonder what she could do with her life that would be meaningful and glorifying to God. In Little Rock she realized she could paint. A teacher awakened and inspired her gift to create beautiful portraits that evoke the soul of the subject.

Not long after Molly had a successful show in her Baton Rouge studio, Barry told me, "Hey, I've got a blessing story for you. I was sent to Little Rock for Molly. I thought (as usual!) that it was about me and so I thought I had made a mistake. But it was about Molly finding her gift and blessing the world with her art. I thought I went there to be blessed. But actually I went to become a blessing. We went through all that stress and worry so Molly could become a painter. And now I realize that's a bigger blessing to me than any success might have been. I'd do it all again in heartbeat."

We have been blessed in order to bless others.[1] The blessing dynamic has never been just about our receiving the blessing of restored communion with God. We know Jesus because someone told us about him. We believed those who told us because we trusted the love that backed up their words. Others who were blessed with salvation carried it forward by blessing us. That means now we have a blessing turn to take. We, too, are sent to bless.

Blessing others generates joy. We get to be in on God's massive re-blessing project in the world. We experience wonder as we realize there is a unique blessing role for each of us to play. The blessing life lights us up with purpose. We get to serve a cause much bigger than ourselves. We participate in being blessers in Christ's name and power. In this third section, we will consider what it means to live to bless in daily life.

The Reach of Aaron's Blessing

As you read Psalm 67 notice how it begins with language from Aaron's powerful name-placing benediction. But then watch for the turn it takes. The prayer asks for God's blessing on the gathered worshipers. But for a reason—so that the blessing will reach to the ends of the earth!

> May God be gracious to us and bless us
> and make his face to shine upon us,
> that your way may be known on earth,
> your saving power among all nations.
> Let the peoples praise you, O God;
> let all the peoples praise you!
>
> Let the nations be glad and sing for joy,
> for you judge the peoples with equity
> and guide the nations upon earth.
> Let the peoples praise you, O God;
> let all the peoples praise you!
>
> The earth has yielded its increase;
> God, our God, shall bless us.
> God shall bless us;
> let all the ends of the earth fear him! (Psalm 67)

A congregation praying this psalm yearns for the shining favor of God upon each life and the whole community assembled. But there's also an understanding that blessed people make good witnesses to the rest of the world that the Lord is truly God and worthy to be served. The psalm says, in other words, "Bless us, God, so that the world will know who you are. Seeing us under your favor, may the whole world realize you are the true God, the righteous judge and the source of all good things." Rejoicing in God's blessing, the congregation desires that all people would praise our God and so enter into the joy of blessing communion.

This prayer for blessing is profoundly missional. The psalm concludes with a joyful summons to people worldwide to acknowledge Israel's blessing God. Aaron's benediction sent the people away from worship with the assurance that they were claimed and protected by God's name. God's presence went with them. In Psalm 67, we see that the people themselves could extend the reach of that blessing through their witness to the world.

This is exactly what Jesus intended as he parted from his disciples. As we considered in the last chapter, Luke's Gospel describes Jesus giving his disciples Aaron's blessing as he ascended. This blessing was meant to fuel and further their mission. Just earlier, Jesus had told them "that repentance and forgiveness of sins should be proclaimed in his name to all nations" (Luke 24:47). Blessing invitations are still being issued. The Father's great welcome in Christ continues. The door is still open to new life. We offer this news as we tell the gospel story. But our words carry weight only when backed by a life characterized by blessing others in speech, in giving, in service. Let's see how this works out for several people in daily life in the world.

Giving Away Your Life

Late one night, a lone lamp is burning in the living room. He thumbs through a magazine but can't keep his mind on it. She is in the bedroom sleeping at last. He is tired—bone-tired—but strangely joyful. Has he ever realized before how much he loves her? Has he ever felt as he does now, when pressing in on every moment is an awareness of how much he wants to be with her? Gutting it out hour by hour in all the daily tasks he must perform, he realizes as never before how much he needs her, now when she needs him most. Yes, he is tired, but there is no quit in him. "I will see it through," he says quietly. The demands of love have made him lean and supple of soul. Even as he weeps for the time that is slipping like sand through his fingers, he knows he wouldn't trade these days for anything. He switches off the light and feels joy like an inextinguishable flame inside him.

A mother, single again, has learned how to be homemaker and financier, breadwinner and hearth-tender in her home. She is disciplinarian and nurturer, yard man and decorator, plumber and seamstress. Every day she does more work than one human being can possibly do, and though she is tired she composes her face with love for her little ones and perseveres. She knows she cannot get sick, can scarcely dream of finding love for herself again, must endure on few touches and even less praise. But she will not fail these children. And in the night God whispers peace. In the day he lends her strength. And after a dozen grinding years that passed in a blur, she realizes how she has been led from shattered heart through bitterness of soul to a renewed softness and beauty. She is more lovely than the untried prettiness of youth. Now she is lit from within with love that does not fail, and beyond hope she counts these years as a joy.

A man wakes after a restless night to the sound of the alarm. For a moment he doesn't know what day it is. Is he in his own room or on the road again? His heart pounds with the insistence of the ring. He rises but can't quite straighten all the way up. It will take a half-hour before he can stretch, and then ten minutes of pain before he's flexible enough to engage the battle of the day. He's too young to retire, too old to be hungry and expectant of much advancement. On the way to his car, he passes his fly fishing rod. In his mind's eye a picture flashes of a secret stream in the mountains, with no one else around and all thoughts and stresses pushed away by the concentration needed to keep the line dancing in its hypnotic rhythm. For two seconds he considers calling in and then taking off.

But people are waiting for him. There are conflicts to be resolved, tangles to be smoothed, customers to satisfy. His pound of flesh is required. They own him from eight to six and demand his blood and sweat every day. Whenever he thinks about tossing his keys on his boss's desk and shouting, "Forget you all!" he thinks of the little bodies sleeping upstairs as he slips out of the garage. They need him employed. And so he perseveres. He endures the trial, denies himself, slogs it out and makes it happen. Day after day he is building a character of reliability. He can be counted on. He is required. And underneath his exhaustion there runs a stream of satisfaction. He has been there and done that for the sake of those he loves. It's really all he ever wanted anyway.

Every day we have opportunity to give ourselves away to bless others. In one sense, blessing costs us nothing less than our whole lives. But rising underneath it all, unexpectedly, is the joy of love. This is what we are meant to do!

Where Will I End Up at Eighty?

My default position in life is to seek my personal comfort and plan my pleasure. (Through rigorous practice, I've actually gotten quite good at this.) Even as I labor to serve the triune God in ministry, I often dream of how I can get free to do what I want. I seek a blessed life in the present age; it's easy to forget that the goal is a blessing life. I join my culture in thinking that if I could just get things arranged right, this world could fulfill me. That's what makes the blessing life so hard. I don't want to give my life away. I don't believe Jesus that in losing my life for him and the gospel I will find it (Mark 8:35).

One way I try to counter my natural inclinations is to consider how I want my life on earth to end up. Do I want to be known as a heavenly or an earthly person? When we're twenty-two and our bodies are strong and the world opens up before the beauty and power of our youth, it's easy to live as if this world is all there is. How often do we see gorgeous young women pouting because the store doesn't have their size in the jeans they wanted for the party?

Or fussing because the drive-through got their order wrong? And those who want to partake of their beauty rush to confirm that this drama matters. How often do we see strong young men competing to take the most out of this life now—to possess the most women, consume the most drink and charm the most money out of those who wish they had such youth again? Thankfully, most of us grow out of such self-focus and gain a larger perspective.

But think about how it could go either way. Imagine ending up at eighty ranting about how the world doesn't revolve around us like it used to, spending all our energy obsessing over trivial slights: "The doctor's office kept me waiting again. The waitress didn't put the dressing on the side of my salad. The mechanic didn't get the clicking out of my engine. The children don't call enough. It's cold in here. No, now I'm burning up. I'm nearly out of money. Everybody's trying to take it from me. The world isn't serving me and I'll just fume about it and make people miserable. Because now is everything. This life is all I have. I want it to be right. Don't people understand?" That's a scary picture to me. But it's just where some of my obsessions and whining will lead.

By contrast, imagine ending up at eighty as someone who sees each person as someone to be blessed. We spend our energy thinking about the lives of the people we know and ponder how we can reach them with love. "That poor doctor is hunted like a fox on the run from the hounds—everybody wants a piece of her. Once I get into the exam room, let me be sure to be thankful. I wonder how the children of my waitress are doing. I think the daughter's name is Sarah. I'll ask. And I'm going to write a note to my children telling them I've been praying for them through the night. I want to be sure my grandson knows how proud I am of him. Did I send a check to those kids on the mission field? I think I can afford a little more. I'm so thankful God has blessed me this long. I'm so thankful Jesus is my Savior. I'm going to heaven soon, but for as long as I'm here, I'm going to thank him."

That's a picture that motivates me. I want to end up so filled with heaven that people can glimpse the farther shores of God's reality whenever they're near me. When they pass me I want them to feel the cool breezes, and when they partake of my life I want them to taste the sweet fruit of God's reality. I don't want to be someone who drags people down into the dirt by idolizing petty concerns as the sum total of reality. I want to be someone who points other people to the Savior by the way I speak and bless and love.

I remember the afternoon I came running into the house excited to tell Rhonda that I'd finally figured out what I wanted to be when I grow up. Really, I'd figured out *who* I want to be. I had just come from meeting Dr. Billings, a retired physician and professor of medicine who was in town visiting family. Now in his mid-nineties, Dr. Billings was intensely interested in others, including me. People still fascinated him. The infirmities of age caused Dr. Billings to spend most of his waking time in a wheelchair, so he had a group of caregivers who helped him with his daily activities. He not only knew their names but their life stories. He traveled (in spite of his disabilities) to visit them across the country. He tried to improve their life situations however he could. I marveled to see someone so passionately other-driven. That focus outside of himself gave Dr. Billings joy. It kept him motivated in living. Though his body confined his movement, he was neither bored nor trapped. Dr. Billings stayed filled with life because he concentrated on other people.

People lit up with blessing others light up the world. Joy wells up from within other-driven people and overflows onto the people with whom they connect. Zest for living energizes them. As we individually follow this blessing path, we learn that there is a communal aspect to blessing as well. God intended his people to affect whole communities with his blessing love.

Seeking the Shalom of the City

For centuries God's people had been told to keep separate from other nations. They were to be a distinctive holy nation whose very difference would draw the world to God. But in 586 B.C., the Babylonians overran the nation and carried away the people. Now in exile, Israel was given a new strategy for engagement with the world:

> Thus says the LORD of hosts, the God of Israel, to all the exiles whom I have sent into exile from Jerusalem to Babylon: Build houses and live in them; plant gardens and eat their produce. Take wives and have sons and daughters. . . . Multiply there, and do not decrease. But seek the welfare of the city where I have sent you into exile, and pray to the LORD on its behalf, for in its welfare you will find your welfare. . . . Your exile will be long; build houses and live in them, and plant gardens and eat their produce. (Jeremiah 29:4-7, 28)

In effect God was saying, "Your nation is lost. The exile will last a lifetime. Don't expect otherwise. The days of your independence and power are over. But your identity as my people remains. Your vocation to bless the world continues. So live in this foreign land with a view toward blessing your captors. Their welfare has become your welfare. Live robustly. Help the prosperity of Babylon by your contributions to a good society. In that way you will be fulfilling my mission and preparing for your return to your homeland."

The implications for the blessing life are striking. We live in a paradox. On the one hand, this world is not our home. Our resting place, our settled place, is yet to come. For now, even if we sleep in the same house for seventy-five years, we still need to consider our lives and possessions as on the road. We can never expect our deepest fulfillment to be here. Exile lasts our whole life in this world. That means God's people will never be able successfully to make this earth our heart's home.

On the other hand, this is the world to which Christ came and for which he died. This is the world to which we are sent. We are to settle here, but not in such a way that we mistake the world for ultimate home. We act as lifelong ambassadors from heaven to the lost and wandering of earth. The Hebrew word translated as "welfare" in Jeremiah 29:7 is the word *shalom*. God's blessing people seek the total well-being of the people around us where we live. We are heralds for God's great re-blessing plan in Christ.

So we pass through this world giving thanks for the blessings of what health, prosperity, love and delight we receive. But we never forget that we are blessed in order to be a blessing. We have been given not in order to stockpile for ourselves but in order to give. We are here to bless the world with the love of God in Christ.

This includes everything from simple good citizenship to direct evangelism, from being helpful neighbors to being innovators in speaking the timeless gospel in a faithful way shaped to these particular times. We are to be honest, smart businesspeople and creative artists of excellence. We are to be great colleagues at work and happy, encouraging recreators in our leisure. We pay our bills on time and we open our hands to the needy. We lead communities to manage natural resources well, to create effective schools and health care for all citizens, to make streets safe and to keep people homed, clothed and fed. We work hard on our marriages and devote ourselves to good parenting. We open wide the doors to our excellent worship and we bring the gospel to the streets. The total prosperity and well-being of our community is our constant focus.[2] Of course, this culture can never fully or finally become the Eden in which we were meant to live. But we seek to make the world we are passing through taste a bit like the home God has promised so others will want to come with us.

Now let's see how this works out in one crucial area of blessing: our speech.

SPEAKING BLESSING

*T*here was a tiny woman in our North Carolina church who had giant spiritual stature in our lives. Miss Jean, as we called her, loved words. She knew that anyone skilled with words possesses great power for both good and ill. When I was a very young pastor, she taught me a verse from Isaiah. And for one with Miss Jean's literary ear, of course it was in the King James Version: "The Lord GOD hath given me the tongue of the learned, that I should know how to speak a word in season to him that is weary" (Isaiah 50:4). She told me that she kept repeating this verse to herself to be reminded of how important our speech is.

The purpose of our tongues is to sustain with good words those who are weary. Paul wrote to the Ephesian church, "Let no corrupting talk come out of your mouths, but only such as is good for building up, as fits the occasion, that is may give grace to those who hear" (Ephesians 4:29). Living to bless means I try to wield my words in a way that never tears down but rather helps construct others in a life of peace and love. We want to give grace to those who hear us speak.

A lovely scene of this kind of blessing speech unfolds in the book of Ruth. Boaz was a landowner who lived in Bethlehem in the days before there were kings in Israel. The time was the harvesting of the barley crop. Boaz arrived at his fields to check the progress of his workers. He hailed his reapers, "The LORD be with you!" (Ruth 2:4). In that simple greeting, Boaz communicated that he understood his life to be part of a much larger purpose than his personal gain. He saw the whole industry of his land as a part of the commonwealth of a community that itself existed to bless the world and glorify God. In striving to realize this vision, owner and workers succeeded or failed together. So Boaz wished the empowering favor of Israel's God upon them.[1]

Boaz's workers replied, "The LORD bless you!" They shared the vision; they trusted the owner. They each understood their individual jobs in light of the whole business of the farm, and they understood the farm in light of the whole plan of God for the world. The harvesters wanted Boaz to be blessed and prosperous, for they were part of his team.

We gather all this merely from overhearing the exchange of blessing. When people invoke God's approving presence among each other in the activities of daily living, they set all of life and work within a deeper context of God's purposes. Moreover, their blessing speech helps to create what it asks for. When we ask for God's presence in another's life, we become aware of how God is already present. We start to notice what God is doing in the world and become open to being part of that divine work. Also, when we bless another, we become more awake to all the people around us. Affection flows between us and makes us more present in our relationships.

So we are not surprised to learn that, perhaps unlike many busy landowners might have done, Boaz noticed a new worker in his field. He inquired about the foreign woman who had come to gather stalks of barley behind the regular reapers.[2] Boaz took particular pains to bless the Moabite woman named Ruth. He told her to stay in his fields where she would be safe. He told her she could drink from the water vessels as if she were one of the permanent workers. He even instructed his men to drop a few extra sheaves for Ruth.

Why such attention to a poor immigrant? In his inquiries, Boaz heard how Ruth had refused to leave her mother-in-law Naomi when the older woman returned to Israel after the deaths of both their husbands. Ruth gave up her homeland, her blood family and even her ancestral gods to join her future to Naomi. In words now well known, Ruth said, "Where you go I will go, and where you lodge I will lodge. Your people shall be my people, and your God my God" (Ruth 1:16).

Those who first heard this story would have noticed the resonance in Ruth's words with the covenant fidelity that God had continually promised to Israel. This foreign woman was not only giving herself to Naomi's God; she embraced God in the very way God had committed to the Hebrews. Ruth's words penetrated to the very heart of God's desire to be with us, expressed when he said, "I will make my dwelling among you. . . . And I will walk among you and will be your God, and you shall be my people" (Leviticus 26:11-12). Ruth the foreigner exhibited the character of the true God. She pledged herself in love to Naomi just as God was joined in love to the people of Israel. Ruth's life was bound up with Naomi's for the rest of her days; God's life is bound up with ours into eternity.

We have seen that Boaz lived and worked in awareness of this covenant-keeping God. So of course he was drawn to Ruth. When the two talked that afternoon, Boaz blessed Ruth: "The LORD repay you for what you have done, and a full reward be given you by the LORD, the God of Israel, under whose wings you have come to take refuge!" (Ruth 2:12). Soon Boaz and Ruth were married. Their son would be the grandfather of David, Israel's great king. And to David God gave an everlasting promise that would be fulfilled in the birth of Jesus Christ, the true King of all kings and Lord of all lords, the long-awaited Son of David. Together Ruth and Boaz formed a union that recovered and displayed the original purpose of the calling of Israel as a particular people: to bless the entire world with God's redeeming presence.

Speaking to One Another

When we hear this story, we are meant to make the connection between the way both people lived out gracious blessing speech and how God brought them together. Blessing others opens opportunities for God's transforming, redeeming power to work.

But these were trained biblical characters. How do we try this at home?

We joked in one Bible study I took part in about what might happen if one of our men walked into a staff meeting, stretched out his arms and declared broadly, "The Lord be with you!" We don't quite have the cultural climate for that now.

But perhaps people in business could begin to think along these lines: *How can I communicate that I desire this coworker's success and happiness? How could I let her know that I will pray for God to bless her? That I will pray God would take care of any personal concerns he has?* As we get intentional about blessing, we can also get creative. People report being amazed when God opens opportunities to say such blessing things as, "I'll pray that God will help you with that." Or, "Wow, that's great how you solved that issue. That really showed the character of God." Smart, intentional blessers in any walk of life who ask God to create blessing moments will always find them.

Paul explained the power of the tongue for destruction or blessing when he wrote, "Let all bitterness and wrath and anger and clamor and slander be put away from you, along with all malice. Be kind to one another, tenderhearted, forgiving one another, as God in Christ forgave you" (Ephesians 4:31-32). I learned part of this passage in church kindergarten. We understood this to be really important. I can still hear our childlike cadence as we recited, "Be ye kind, one to another." That's not theologically complicated. But it's very powerful. Just be kind. That's a crucial step in Living to Bless. If nothing else, we just:

- Stop being mean and start being nice.

- Stop being indifferent and be kind enough to notice.

- Stop being surly and offer encouragement.

- Stop being distant and draw close.

- Stop being distracted and pay attention.

Dr. Billings, whom we met last chapter, told me he'd had a powerful experience of conviction about his words on a Sunday when he went to worship with one of his caregivers. Though the church was huge, he felt that the preacher was speaking directly to him. He said the minister preached a very simple sermon. It had one key message. "Don't complain! Don't complain! Don't complain!" Though I had never heard him complain, Dr. Billings felt convicted of a self-focus on his pains and troubles. He knew the antidote was in speech that built up others.

I had an experience of the power of such constructive talk from someone who had every right to be moaning. It happened on what seemed like our 965th trip up the tower elevator in Our Lady of the Lake Hospital. My brother and I were going to visit our father during his monthlong stay. We made idle conversation with the woman who shared the elevator with us. Then, following an impulse, I asked her, "Do you have somebody here?"

"My grandson," she replied. "He's fifteen and he's gone blind."

"Oh, I'm sorry," I said. "That's so tough."

"God is good, all the time," she returned. Then, as the elevator opened, she started to walk out but turned around and said, "God is good. I don't mean tomorrow. I mean today. Right now, God is good and I praise him for that."

The doors closed and she was gone. I never saw her again, but her words stayed with me. Her praise was not a pious platitude. And in case we might have mistaken her earnestness, she had turned to make her declaration clear. Even now, even with a teenager who'd lost his sight, she knew that God was good in this very present moment. There's power in such testimony. Because it's real. She well could have been focused on worry for her grandson, but she chose to use her tongue to bless God and then us. She connected life in this hour to the eternal God. And I still feel the power of that moment.

Linking People to Jesus

We may hesitate to bless others when we just don't know what to say, so we can develop blessing speech by getting the language of Scripture more and more on our lips and our keyboards. The power for blessing is in God's Word. Sometimes we can offer it directly and other times in paraphrase. People are not often receptive to prescription advice from God, but today there is a great openness to stories. So what could happen if we sent or spoke snippets of stories from Jesus' interactions with people? Then we could add our own prayers that Jesus would speak the same way to those whom we wish to bless. For example, as Jesus walked across the water to his terrified, wave-tossed disciples, he said, "Take heart; it is I. Do not be afraid" (Mark 6:50). We might be sent to people trembling in the rolling seas of life with the news, "The Lord is with you. Christ is in this storm, and he remains the lord of all winds and seas. Take courage."

In Jesus' parable about a father's great love for his two sons, he graciously told the resentful elder brother, "Son, you are always with me, and all that is mine is yours" (Luke 15:31). Perhaps we can speak blessing to those who feel they have been treated unfairly, who have grown bitter over life: "The Lord is always with you. Nothing has been withheld. God's gracious hand is still open to you. Receive that love."

Before he ascended, Jesus gave his disciples the mission of going out to all the world. Then he said, "And behold, I am with you always, to the end of the age" (Matthew 28:20). We have much to undertake in engaging the world with the blessing love of Emmanuel. We can encourage each other by saying, "The Lord goes with you, all the way to the end of the line. Going in Christ's name, you never go alone."

Blessing speech has powerful effects. It's not a native language for many of us, but we may learn to speak it in little increments. Lately, I've been closing many emails and letters with the words, "With you in Christ, Gerrit." In other words, "The Lord is with us. We are in Christ, so I am with you and for you through the one who has come to be with and for us."

"We Bless You from the House of the LORD"

I have always loved the cover of Bruce Springsteen's first album. It's drawn like a postcard, the kind you might send home from a vacation at the beach, with the words, "Greetings from Asbury Park." It made me wonder what it would have been like to have been at the Stone Pony on the New Jersey shore, hearing Bruce and the E Street Band before they were stars. Imagine being close to that passion and energy. The album title makes me feel like Bruce wanted to share that with us: "Hey, we came from Asbury Park; we got it going out there, and we were all into the music when we thought of you. Here's a taste of what we heard and felt."

There's a verse from Psalm 118 that creates the same feeling in me. It says, "We bless you from the house of the LORD" (Psalm 118:26). We're here in the sanctuary of our God. We've got it going. The music is lifting us into his presence. The Word is challenging us and changing us. Communion is binding us to Jesus and one another. Our fellowship is encouraging us. And while we're here, we're thinking of you. Wish you were here. We bless you from the house of the Lord! We want you with us. We want you to know this joy that we know. From our gathering, we extend not just our greetings but the blessing of our God to you.

So we actually tried that at our church. We put a postcard of our sanctuary in every bulletin. On the back we printed, "We bless you from the house of the Lord!" At the end of the service I asked everyone to consider who might need to hear that encouragement from us today. Then we took a few minutes right in the pews to jot our notes. I encouraged people to mail their cards, slip them under a door or put them on a pillow. The idea was to link to the blessing ripple that came from Ruth and Boaz. We keep the blessing speech going.

Spoken Blessings

Bill Gothard has a wonderful little book called *The Power of Spoken Blessings*. In it he says,

> We can not only experience that life-lifting, joy-charged encouragement from heaven; we actually direct that powerful flow into the hearts of others. Like the worker at the controls of a canal, we can open the floodgates and let the strong river of God's grace surge through us as we bless people in his mighty name.
>
> So we see that the power our spoken blessings flows first of all from the abundance of our Creator's own blessedness— and from His wise and loving intention to bless His children

with whatever is truly our highest good. When we verbalize a blessing upon others, we have the privilege of taking part in channeling God's goodness to them and in directing them to the Lord's will.

That's why our strongest blessings to others will come when we invoke the mighty name of God, for that name designates His personality, His character, His will, and His heart for blessing all creation. The most powerful blessings begin, then, by simply speaking His name: "The Lord bless you."[3]

We can get in on this kind of blessing in stages. First, we begin by praying for people in the form of a blessing from Scripture. Then, once we have blessed them with scriptural benedictions in our own prayers, we go on to write them those words. Finally, when we get bold, we can actually offer to pray those words over them.

The more facility we develop in blessing speech, the more we can actually blend Scripture's words with our words to give a blessing unique to the situations people face. We can follow the pattern of Aaron's benediction while bringing in specific prayer requests. Gothard gives this example:

> May the Lord God bless you and keep you from the torment of fear and anxiety. May He cause His face to shine upon you with power, love and a sound mind and give you grace to cast out fear through perfect love. May He lift up His countenance upon you with freedom as you tell Him every detail of your need in earnest, thankful prayer, and give you the peace that surpasses all understanding, as He keeps your heart and mind safe through Jesus Christ.[4]

Such a simple prayer has remarkable power. If we dare to offer to pray this way, we become the bridge between our blessing God and the people we love. God has branded us with his blessing love. We hear it whenever we gather in his house. So we go on to bless others from the house of the Lord. We link God's intentions for his people with specific people and their needs. We can each know the joy of blessing in God's name.

Now, I suspect that you may already be thinking, *I'll never do this. I can't. It's too weird. I don't know enough Scripture.* Don't get stuck there! You can write out a blessing like this and then read it to someone. We all want a Christianity that is more effective, more meaningful and more joyful. It is available through blessing. We can speak to one other more deeply, more powerfully than we have ever imagined. Lives will change as we do so. Who might you be called to bless this very week? Ask God to show you. Make a plan to engage in blessing speech. It may be through an email, a text, a phone call, a letter or a visit. You just may be the only one who can give someone that gift.

14

ON THE CONTRARY, BLESS

ᖇᖇ

*F*or years my son Jacob and I have played a running game of "I got you last!" Chances are you've played it before. Someone touches you and says "I got you last." It could be a smack on the arm or a feather-light stroke of the neck. It doesn't matter. If you've played for a while, the announcement itself becomes meaningless. Simply any contact means you were got last. That fact burns into the brains of your competitors. You have to get the other guy back. Because the universe is out of balance. It will only be put right if you can get him—no matter where you are or who's around. We always found church services, piano recitals and school plays to be excellent venues for the game. Making the touch while everyone else is still and quiet creates a delicious challenge.

The game continues because retaliation is ingrained in our brains. Watch toddlers play. "You take my truck; I take it back. You pull my hair; I'm going to throw sand in your face. If you're too big and scary, I'll go tell the teacher. That'll fix you." In elementary school if you called me a name, I learned to reply, "I know you are, but what am I?" Or we would hold up our palms like a mirror: "What you say is what you are!" Getting back is as natural and normal as breathing.

Living to bless, however, is unnatural, especially at first. Christianity runs contrary to human inclination. Turning the other cheek after being struck or answering an insult with a kindness goes against our grain. But such counterintuitive actions are distinctive to the followers of Jesus. Let's consider several passages where blessing in the face of being cursed is affirmed in the New Testament.

Reflecting Sadness and Joy, Absorbing Venom

In Romans 12, Paul teaches that we are to be responsive to each other in love. We empathize with someone's suffering so that we actually "weep with those who weep." We embrace the success of another to the point that we "rejoice with those who rejoice" (Romans 12:15). The work of love can be to reflect back with our own feelings what someone is going through. We're called to mirror another's joy or sadness.

But in the case of venomous cursing, we are not to bounce it back. Anger is one of the most contagious emotions, but we are to be inoculated against it. We are to absorb hostility and return blessing. So Paul said in this same section, "Bless those who persecute you; bless and do not curse them. . . . Do not be overcome by evil, but overcome evil with good" (Romans 12:14, 21). We are to be exceptionally reactive to people in pain or joy. We are to be exceptionally disengaged from their emotions when they are hostile, reflecting back only a reply of love. As we do, we look for the deeper emotion under the rage, such as fear, betrayal or abandonment, to which we may respond empathically.

Failing to save face by retaliation seems ridiculous if we live normally by the law of the jungle, the law of the playground or the law of the corporate arena. Peter says it starkly: "Do not repay evil for evil or reviling for reviling, but on the contrary, bless" (1 Peter 3:9). On the contrary, bless. When we get slapped, dissed or snapped at, we reply by wishing them well. On the contrary to what our insides are screaming out to do, we bless instead.

Peter goes on to confirm these instructions and issue a promise: "Bless, for to this you were called, that you may obtain a blessing" (1 Peter 3:9). If we are called to Christ, we are summoned to a way of life that appears oddly, ridiculously unnatural. But this is the real guts of the blessing life. And Peter tells us that reflecting grace in the face of cursing is the guaranteed way into experiencing the blessing of God. His favor, provision and powerful eternal life flow more dynamically through us in situations where we act in love contrary to natural impulse.

The Way of Christ

Jesus not only taught this way of blessing, he lived it as no one ever had. He took the blows and the crown of thorns from the soldiers without rebuking them. He took the sentence of Pilate without protest. He remained on the cross instead of calling the legions of angels that were at his disposal (Matthew 26:53). Jesus lived what he preached as he gave himself into the hands of evil that the world might be redeemed. How did he do it? His response of love had everything to do with knowing the true character of his heavenly Father. Let's recall some of what he said:

> But I say to you who hear, Love your enemies, do good to those who hate you, bless those who curse you, pray for those who abuse you. . . . As you wish that others would do to you, do so to them. . . . Love your enemies, and do good, and lend, expecting nothing in return, and your reward will be great, and you will be sons of the Most High, for he is kind to the ungrateful and the evil. Be merciful, even as your Father is merciful. (Luke 6:27, 31, 35-36)

Love your enemies. Pray for them. Do good to them. That's the blessing life. It's counterintuitive. And Jesus spoke to people who did not have a lot of extra resources for this. His followers by and large did not have a lot of education, economic options or political freedom. He addressed people who had been abused, squashed, squeezed, cast off, judged and dismissed. Still he told them, "Bless those who curse you. Love your enemies." People with very few earthly resources could draw from the inexhaustible resources of steadfast love and kindness in the heavenly Father. So how do we live from this source?

Two Qualifications

Before we jump into how we love our enemies, I want to give two qualifications related to acute cases of abuse. First, it's very important to emphasize right away that Jesus is not saying you should continue to offer yourself to be beaten, raped, robbed or bullied. It is not loving someone to allow them to continue to be a perpetrator of violence or theft against you. That keeps them in their sickness and sin even as it keeps you being injured. Seek help. Thankfully, in this country no one has to remain a victim. There are people who can help you. God does not want this kind of life for you. It is not happening because you somehow deserve this violence. A life of abuse is not normal and should not be accepted as your due.

Second, there may be a time lag between understanding the need to bless the enemy and actually being able to do it. If you think you can forgive immediately when great harm has been done to you, you are minimizing the reality of what's going on deep in your soul. There is a lot of hurt and then anger to be uncovered when you have been sorely wounded by an enemy. Forgiveness is not instant, nor is it easy. Dan Allender is a psychologist who works with adults who were sexually abused as children. He notes that a turning point in the healing process comes months into the therapy when he asks, "Imagine if you had a button in your hand that, if you pushed it, would send your abuser to everlasting hell. Would you push it?"[1] The day the person says "No, I would not send him to hell" is the first glimmer of forgiveness that is real and on the way. It takes time.

It is true that Jesus calls us to love and pray even for those enemies who have harmed us to the very marrow of our souls. And the dynamic of forgiveness and blessing is the same for these soul enemies as well as for those who are simply a nuisance. But we recognize that acute abuse calls for seeking immediate shelter and that forgiveness of acute abuse takes more time and more hard work.

That said, this chapter is primarily concerned with the more usual enemies and cursers we face. Ordinary betrayers. Common deceivers. Liars. Slanderers. Smotherers. High demanders. Garden-variety sickos who want to paste their illness onto you. People working out their family dynamics at your expense. Jealous enviers who don't want you to succeed. People who want what you have. Enviers who would like to see you fall. Criticizers and critiquers. The "my way or the highway" crowd. Random angry people who spew their venom your way. You know the folks I mean. How do we draw from the Father's love in order bless and love them?

No More Rent-Free Head Space

We realize that by far the most power people exercise in our lives is mental more than physical. It's not just their words or actions in the moment, which are really not pleasant, it's the way we keep thinking about what they said or did. The enemy's power is not as much in the tip of the sword that pierces our skin as it is in the poison on the end of that blade that gets in our bloodstream. I can think about confrontations I've had with people in traffic more than a year ago and get my blood boiling and heart pounding right now. "Why I shoulda told that guy . . . " Then I realize he's still exercising power over me. Now consider how much someone really threatened me or hit close to my true heart and, well, when I was writing this section it took a huge discipline not to go off thinking for an hour about these enemies and how evil they are.

I have a friend in North Carolina who has done a lot of work dealing with people who have hurt him in the past. He's learned to realize the link between addictions he struggles with and the hurt that he experienced. One time I was going on and on about someone who was acting like an enemy toward me and how awful this guy was. My friend listened for a while, then spoke in his long, slow western Carolina cadence, "Gerrit, you're letting that guy live in your head."

"I know, Jack. He just barged into my head. He's made himself at home."

"But Gerrit, you're letting him live in your head rent-free! Don't do it. You've got to evict him."

Exactly. The worst power most of our enemies have over us is mental. We nurse our hurts and replay the terrible words over and over. We get shocked and outraged all over again every day. We compose replies. We fantasize victories. We plead our cause before a judge and win again and again. We refuse to forgive and thereby keep the sin alive and kicking in our souls. The other person may never even give us another thought. We are punishing and torturing only ourselves. We're giving rent-free residence to our enemies. Why, we fluff their pillows and put chocolates on the bedside table for them! We urge them to stay and we pick up the tab. We pay in the currency of our health, our ragged emotions, our bitterness and misery. "Gerrit, you've got to evict him."

That's where the wisdom of Jesus comes in. I hate to pray for enemies. But Jesus knew what he was talking about. It's the path to freedom. It stops the pain. It ends the war. It takes power away from the enemy. It brings God and his healing presence to bear. It invites the heavenly sheriff to come into your house and evict the squatters.

Now I can hear you thinking, like me, *Oh, sure, I'll pray for her. Pray that she gets a horrible disease and dies!* No, that's not going to do it. So what do I pray? Well, I know I don't have it in me to wish this person well. So I have to tap into the love of our blessing God. I look at Jesus' words, "Be merciful, even as your Father is merciful" (Luke 6:36), and "He is kind to the ungrateful and the evil" (Luke 6:35). I acknowledge that I am a sinner in need of mercy. I am ungrateful and evil. Yet my Father is merciful to me. So I ask him to be just as merciful to my enemy as he is to me. It might look like this:

> Father, I know you do not repay me according to what I deserve but according to your grace in Jesus Christ. So act toward this enemy in the same grace. I don't know how to pray for him. I can't really wish him well. But I can pray that your will would be done in his life. I pray you would be at work in his heart. I will not try to prescribe to you what that work is, even though if you wanted my advice, I have some great ideas. Rather, I will just say, Father, complete the good work you began in him. Bring your truth to bear. Bring your Word to fulfillment. Be God in his life. Be the triune God of grace toward him, according to your plan.

Perhaps you have to go on to deal with the fact that you are holding onto the sin committed against you by the enemy. You are treating this evil as if it were a possession you have the right to own and cherish and finger and obsess over. So your prayers might have to follow along these lines:

> Father, I have been hurt. That betrayal was a deep one. Those words were like daggers. That theft has left me nearly broke. That abandonment has emptied me and left me with nothing

but ashes in my mouth. And I confess that I want to hold onto
this pain. If I let it go, my need might get overlooked. If I give
it up, this sinner might go free and not have justice. I want to
hold this pain so I can cry out, "Look, I've been wronged!"

But Jesus I know that you bought and paid for my sins in
your blood. You also bought the sins of the person who harmed
me. These sins against me belong to you. You gave your life to
purchase them. I don't get to keep them unless I want to keep
the guilt of my own sin too and go to the hell of separation
from you. I want mercy more than I want justice—for myself
and for the one who hurt me. I will stop wrestling you for possession of these wounds. They are yours. Forgive. Bind up.
Take what you have bought and transform us, Lord Jesus.

Such prayers change us. When we can do that with the "big"
enemies who have hurt us, we can readily become blessers of the
smaller, daily enemies we all face. Through such prayer we begin
to realize we possess nothing. We own nothing. We control nothing.
It all belongs to Jesus, who bought not only our sins but our very
lives. We belong to him. He gives us all we need and more.
Therefore, when something is taken away I do not rage because he
has allowed it. He has not left me, and I owned nothing to begin
with. It was borrowed as a gift and now it's being used elsewhere.
Our words toward our enemy might look like this:

You spoke ugly words to me. It feels unfair. But I know you
cannot even begin to speak the depth of my wickedness. Only
God knows the truest truth about me. And he has bought all
my evil for his own. He who knows me best calls me his beloved. He has sealed me for eternal life. You cannot actually
curse me, for I am kept in the blessing of God, so I bless you
back. Poor thing, bless your heart for thinking your words
can touch my identity in Christ. No, dear, you don't have that

power. He owns me and he has set his name on me. It's just silly to think you could touch that with your puny words. God bless you with news of his love.

I acknowledge that this is a strange way to think. It's unnatural. But it's also real. Powerful. Liberating. On the contrary, bless. We've got to practice to be ready to do this. We anticipate and plan to bless first rather than retaliate. The wonder is that this way of loving holds true in even the direst circumstances. It has the power to utterly transform evil into good.

The Power of Blessing Forgiveness

When my family and I arrived in Baton Rouge, we soon met David and Coco Treppendahl. They had been members of our church for many years until they moved to a neighboring town, but they stayed close to their old friends. People told us that our sanctuary was never so full as it was during their daughter Laura's funeral. She had been killed by a drunk driver before she was twenty-one years old. The young man driving the fatal vehicle was a fellow student of Laura's at Old Miss. Soon after we met them, David told me about the power of forgiveness.

The Treppendahls did not press charges against the driver. In fact, they went in person to offer him their forgiveness. Then they wrote the judge who would be handling the sentencing after the trial. Here is an excerpt:

Your Honor:

We appreciate the opportunity to convey our sentiments to you regarding the sentencing. . . . We are Christians. Forgiveness is an integral part of our Christian faith. We have asked Christ and He has enabled us to fully forgive . . . the young man involved in this tragedy. Therefore, from our own personal perspective, we have no need for nor will we gain any satisfaction from seeing him further punished.

The Treppendahls saw no reason why this young man should lose his life through years of incarceration. They understood what it is to be young and foolish. They knew that revenge would not bring the healing of Christ.

The judge did indeed give a minimum sentence. The young man who had been wracked with shame and guilt experienced powerful grace. He realized that because the Treppendahls could forgive him, he could believe that God would be forgiving too. Soon after the trial the young man received Christ as his Savior and Lord.

The power in forgiveness is stunning. It also ripples way beyond the moment. Friends of the driver who were in the courtroom were profoundly moved by David Treppendahl's letter pleading for leniency. Hearts were softened throughout their fraternity. Many became Christians, the kind of believers who want to extend Christ's love in daily life and in mission trips around the world.

Losing a child is about as bad as it gets. Two grieving parents could have been justifiably enraged. They could have gone on a vengeful quest for justice, seeking to curse the perpetrator for the rest of his life. But contrary to normal instinct, they blessed instead. Through forgiving the driver their own bitterness was lifted. But even more, there was also salvation for one shattered man and then dozens more. The grace of Christ they passed on continues to bless people a decade later.

One of the benefits of doing the work to receive God's blessing and to bless him back is that we fill our thoughts with all our God has done for us. Through such praise, desire actually gets awakened in us to live from God's mercy and grace. We are urged to give all power, all demands, all control up to God. We own nothing. He has bought us, bought the sins we committed and the sins committed against us. We are his possession, beloved and cherished. We belong to the King of kings who laid aside his glory and died for those who were still his enemies (Romans 5:10). In him, in that faith alone, we can learn the tremendous, magnificent, liberating freedom of the words, "On the contrary, bless."

15

BLESSING BEYOND OURSELVES

❦

*N*ancy came upstairs from the school that occupies our children's area during the week. She said, "I had a sweet time of prayer last night. God reminded me of what he said to me years ago: 'Take care of my children.' For years I kept asking, 'Who are the children you mean?' I thought it might be the kids in Sunday school, or the kids I taught at the private school, or the kids I tutored, or my own kids. Then one day I was driving through the Gardere neighborhood and I heard his voice. It was clear and audible: 'These are my children.'"

Gardere is one of the toughest neighborhoods in Baton Rouge. Nearly all the children raised there are at risk for poverty, drug abuse or violence. And Nancy Zito had a vision to create a Christian school for families in Gardere. At first I thought the idea was noble but not really possible. How could we fund a school? How could we untangle the Gordian knot of problems such children have? But Nancy persisted. She began with an after-school tutoring program at a church in Gardere. We saw the transformation that persistent love can bring about. The parents urged us to go forward with the vision. They wanted a better future for their children.

And now Nancy and her board are in their second year of the school's existence. Last year there were twelve students; this year there are thirty. They come to our church while the board finds property in Gardere and gets a permanent school in place. Already every student has advanced at least one extra grade level. And they are learning the blessing story of the Bible along with their other subjects.

But it's not easy. In my office that day Nancy continued, "A couple of weeks ago, I was ready to shut down the whole school. It just seemed like more than we could handle. So many problems! But God gives me strength. He just keeps reminding me, 'These are my children. I claim them.'"

As we talked, a little boy was sitting outside the office. He had been acting out the chaos of his home life and was not able to get along in the classroom. "God reminded me that this one too is one of the children he claims," Nancy said. "I have to persist for his children."

Living to bless can take us into some difficult regions, to places we don't expect. But if we follow Jesus' priorities, the blessing life will nearly always lead us to children.

Taking Them in His Arms

At one point in his ministry Jesus issued a high-priority invitation: "Let the children come to me; do not hinder them, for to such belongs the kingdom of God" (Mark 10:14). Mark's Gospel describes a great blessing scene that followed: "And he took them in his arms and blessed them, laying his hands on them" (Mark 10:16). The Greek word more literally means Jesus enfolded the children in his arms. Can you visualize the scene? Jesus extends his arms towards the children, then folds up his arms close to himself, now full of little ones. He gathers them. He scoops them up. Then, balancing the children on his lap or hip, Jesus puts his hands on the children as he blesses them. I feel sure Jesus repeated his actions until he had held, touched and blessed every child offered to him.

What do you imagine Jesus said as he blessed the children? Perhaps he repeated the words his Father had said to him: "You are my beloved Son" (Mark 1:11; 9:7). Or maybe he made personal to the children what he had said as a principle to his disciples: "To you belongs the kingdom of heaven." He could have said something like his words in John 10:27: "My sheep hear my voice, and I know them, and they follow me." Or maybe he spoke the blessing with words from an episode recorded by Matthew: "It is not the will of my Father who is in heaven that one of [you] little ones should perish" (Matthew 18:14). Or, "[Your] angels always see the face of my Father who is in heaven" (Matthew 18:10). We may be sure the blessing included words of life and love. If Aaron's upraised hands in blessing indicated a branding of the people with the name of God, how much more did the touch of Jesus' hands on the heads of the little ones mark them as his Father's own?

This scene reminds me of the beautiful commendation prayer spoken at Anglican funerals: "Acknowledge, we humbly beseech thee, a sheep of thine own fold, a lamb of thine own flock, a sinner of thine own redeeming."[1] We all want to be children in the arms of Jesus receiving such a blessing. Indeed, the hope is that each of us would receive deeply that claiming, blessing love offered to us in Jesus.

But the point now is that Jesus showed particular interest in children. He was in serious earnest about the way we adults treat these dependent little ones. Children were a high priority to Christ. So how does that connect to the blessing life?

Blessing Our Children

Blessing is one of the primary ways parents love their children. Especially important is our verbal blessing of their acceptance and favor. As we have often seen, Scripture teaches the importance of a positive action by describing the effects of its opposite. In Genesis 28–29, we read how Jacob tricked his father Isaac into giving the blessing of the firstborn to him instead of Esau, the rightful older brother. As we read the words Esau cried out, we realize this episode is about much more than getting material possessions as an inheritance. The son is crying out for his father's favor. In his despair, he futilely tries to claim his father again and again, begging for acknowledgment as a son. We read, "Bless me, even me also, O my father. . . . Have you but one blessing, my father? Bless me, even me also, O my father" (Genesis 27:34, 38). The text says then that "Esau lifted up his voice and wept" (Genesis 27:38). The grief of not receiving his father's blessing pierced the young man to his heart.

Few of us can stand to live continually in the pain of such grief. Pain has to become something else to be manageable, so it often turns to anger. So we read next, "Now Esau hated Jacob because of the blessing with which his father had blessed him." He vowed, "I will kill my brother Jacob" (Genesis 27:41). The young man would carry hatred and violence in his heart for decades before he found peace.

We know that the rage in young men even today often has at its root a deep blessing wound. Former NFL player Bill Glass has spent decades working in prison ministry around the country with thousands of inmates. He has discovered that the vast majority of male prisoners have never experienced the blessing of their fathers. Glass says, "Unless you feel like the father, the progenitor, has blessed you, you just don't feel like you're worth very much." This pain becomes anger that becomes a desperate, destructive lashing out. Glass has concluded that "the cause of criminality is the lack of the father's blessing."[2]

In his messages, Glass urges both mothers and fathers to bless their children, no matter how old they've gotten. It's crucial for parents to communicate blessing to their children by claiming them in love. And in particular, because it has been historically so lacking, Glass notes how vital it is for fathers to bless sons. He urges parents to "grab 'em and hug 'em and bless 'em."

A simple message of blessing—"You're mine and I'm glad. You're a winner and I'm proud of you. I love you and I think you're terrific"—can move both parents and children to grateful tears. I can testify personally to the powerful bonding such words create with children. Blessing releases joy; it ushers families into the freedom of acceptance. It creates confidence strong enough to face adversity. It motivates for success far more than any negative nagging. Blessing our children communicates deep, unshakeable love.

Interestingly, Glass notes how few inmates in our prison system are Jewish—far fewer than the general population percentages might indicate. His theory links the long tradition of Jewish fathers blessing their children with an extraordinarily low crime rate. The reason is that "the old Jewish fathers know how to gather their sons and daughters close to them, and kiss 'em and bless 'em." Indeed, it is a Jewish custom still practiced in many households for the father to speak Aaron's blessing over his children on the evening of the Sabbath. I have heard men witness as to how formative this blessing rite has been to them.

We have here two ways, then, to bless our children: 1) Bless them with assurance of our love as parents, and 2) Bless them with assurance of God's love and blessing upon them. Both are needed.

If you have young children or grandchildren, here's a great way to start blessing. Put your hands on their back or head, or just hug them close, and pray Aaron's blessing for them. Say their names as you speak God's name. "The LORD bless you and keep you, the LORD make his face to shine upon you." And then, of course, you can add your own words of love and blessing. They will love the affection, and you will be literally binding God's name to their lives. You might want to practice first with your spouse. It's hard to overcome our hesitancy, but the results will quickly reward our daring.

Loving the Least of These

But not all of us have children. And there are a lot more children in need of blessing than there are parents able and willing to bless them. In fact, there are more than 163 million orphans worldwide. Jesus gave high priority to blessing children. How will we respond?

In the last week of his life, Jesus told a blessing parable that is devastatingly convicting. In the story he describes the last judgment in which he as king will divide people as a farmer separates the sheep from the goats. One group is extolled for feeding, clothing and visiting the great king. They have lived the blessing life on earth and will receive eternal life in heaven. "Come, you who are blessed by my Father, inherit the kingdom prepared for you from the foundation of the world" (Matthew 25:34). These blessed "sheep" do not remember rendering such service to the king. He will explain, "Truly, I say to you, as you did it to one of the least of these my brothers, you did it to me" (Matthew 25:40). The other group, the "goats," will be sentenced to eternal punishment. Not because they got their theology wrong but because they failed to care for the king. They, too, will be baffled as to when such neglect occurred. The king will say, "Truly, I say to you, as you did not do it to one of the least of these, you did not do it to me" (Matthew 25:45).

I have to say, this parable scares the willies out of me. For all the theology I know about salvation by grace alone through faith alone, I certainly don't want to be standing before the king saying, "Well, I thought that since Jesus gave me his righteousness, I didn't really need to care for the least and lost. I figured you had that all taken care of." Only Jesus can overcome our sin and estrangement from

God. His blessing of forgiveness is pure gift. But his summons for us to reflect that blessing to others, especially the least, is a clarion call. It matters.

Thankfully, Christ's church worldwide is mounting a huge effort to care for the children Jesus loves. Not everyone will be called all the way to the kind of school Nancy Zito runs. But any of us can participate. Here are a few blessing ideas:

- Buying supplies for classrooms in poorer school districts.

- Helping to fill backpacks with food and school supplies for at-risk children to take home over the weekend.

- Sponsoring a child through a world relief organization.

- Sending shoeboxes of gifts and clothes around the world through the Samaritan Purse Operation Shoe Box program.

- Partnering your church with a local school, adopting classes and blessing the school in any way needed.

- Partnering with a church across the globe and finding ways to care for the children in that community.

- Participating in local tutor or mentoring programs.

- Offering a ReCess program at your church by which parents of special needs children receive a night out and volunteers receive the blessing of being with these children.

- Creating a summer sports camp for at-risk children in your community.

- Becoming a Big Brother or Big Sister, a foster parent or an adoptive parent.

I have watched Christ's people come up with wonderful, creative ways to bless children and families. One man created a ministry called Together for Adoption. This ministry teaches the deep, affirming truths of our adoption in Christ while raising awareness of how to care for orphans worldwide. A woman in our church created Manners of the Heart to teach the connection between good manners, loving relationships and success in life. Another created a ministry called Threads of Love to provide garments for stillborn and aborted children to be buried in. Still another is starting a Christian school in the middle of a difficult neighborhood.[3] The opportunities are endless. There is work suited to every age, skill, temperament and budget. The need and call are shimmeringly clear: the blessing life means intentionally caring for children. Like Jesus, we too can extend our arms to the children and gather them close, enfolding them in blessing. Our watchword can be his own: "Let the children come to me."

GIVING TO BLESS

∽

$\mathscr{B}$efore the storm hit in full force, we lost power in our home in Baton Rouge, Louisiana. So we listened to the news about Hurricane Katrina on a scratchy transistor radio. For almost half a day, it appeared that New Orleans had been spared the worst. Then the levees broke and the city went under water. The nation's heart turned toward the Gulf Coast. A flood of giving from God's people rushed to counter the flood of disaster.

Power came back on at our church before most places, so we became a hub for relief efforts. People pulled off the interstate, came to our door and said, "God told me I should stop here and help. What can I do?" We still shake our heads in wonder as we ask, "Did you ever get that guy's name who took the night shift that crazy Thursday? He was like an angel. He came, did what was desperately needed, then he was gone."

While New Orleans remained closed, Baton Rouge provided a staging ground for workers. Some seventy-five US Marshalls made our church gymnasium their home for several weeks. (Yes, we felt very safe during those chaotic days.) People started washing sheets and clothes for them. Meanwhile teams went over to the River

Center, our local convention center that had been turned into a huge shelter for hurricane refugees. We visited, prayed, played games and smiled a lot. It's a surprisingly important ministry just to relieve the boredom and tension of those who have had to flee their homes and wait in a great hall with nothing to do. A number of us scooped up families and brought them to our homes. One Saturday our youth leaders organized a huge festival for the children on the lawn outside the center.

People gave. Churches all over the country called us. They said, "We know you; we trust you; can we send you a check for relief work?" More than half a million dollars passed through our hands on the way to rebuild. Once New Orleans reopened, thousands of Christians poured into the city to begin the massive cleanup and restoration. The effort continues more than seven years later. Our friends at Trinity Christian Community Center, for instance, have marshaled volunteers from around the nation and have, to date, rebuilt more than three hundred homes in their neighborhood. There is no end in sight. I understand that government played a big role; I know that people of different faith and no faith contributed, too. But anybody who was on the ground in those months knows that the church of Jesus Christ was and remains overwhelmingly the leader in getting the work done.

Enriched for Generosity

The blessing life is the giving life. Those who belong to Jesus Christ understand that we belong to one another as well. Organically linked by the Spirit, we care for one another as family. The Spirit also pushes us beyond the walls of the church. The joy of living with open, blessing hands causes us to reach toward any in need. While giving is not limited to money, our financial resources are a key focus for blessing received and shared.

I have said rather strongly that we have no guarantees of material blessings when it comes to the blessing life. Biblically, we cannot make any one-to-one correspondence between the blessings of prosperity promised to Israel upon obedience in the Promised Land and what we can expect as faithful Christians today. We actually have more in common with Israel in exile than Israel in the land. As sojourners, we are making no permanent homes in this world. We determine to be content with mere travel provisions, daily bread, as we pass through. That's our pilgrim perspective on material blessings.

But that does not mean that God never blesses his people with earthly prosperity. Indeed, anyone who lives in the United States has access to abundance that kings of old would have envied. A good education and hard work do quite often lead to financial bounty. We pilgrims partake of such tangible blessings with joy. If we don't confuse them with our ultimate goals, we may enjoy them as gifts. As we do, we give thanks to the triune God as the source of all good things. In fact, many of Christ's people are entrusted with great amounts of wealth. But to what end are we so blessed?

There are two principles of giving in the Deuteronomy blessing passages that apply to us as New Testament believers as we engage the blessing life. We will see them both picked up in the teachings of Jesus and Paul.

God's gift undergirds all we earn by work. Moses warned the people before they entered the land, "Beware lest you say in your heart, 'My power and the might of my hand have gotten me this wealth.' You shall remember the LORD your God, for it is he who gives you power to get wealth, that he may confirm his covenant" (Deuteronomy 8:17-18).

We have a choice when hard work brings us good wages. We can say, "I did it; I did it all." Or we can say, "Thank you, God, for this blessing that followed my labor. You are the source of everything." The one looks at prosperity as a right and a possession. The other looks at it as a gift in which we were privileged to participate. A downturn sends the "self-made" worker hunkering down in panic. "Oh no! What happened? I'd better protect myself. I could lose it all." The blesser, by contrast, looks at the smaller harvest and says, "This will be enough. I trust your provision. You will fill in what I need even after I give some to those who have none." Jesus told the parable of the rich fool who had a great harvest. His response was not to give but to hoard. He tore down his old barns and built new ones to house all his grain. Then he had a chat with himself: "Soul, you have ample goods laid up for many years; relax, eat, drink, be merry" (Luke 12:19). In other words, he thought it was all for him. Jesus continued, "But God said to him, 'Fool! This night your soul is required of you, and the things you have prepared, whose will they be?'" (Luke 12:20). The fool died alone sitting on a heap of wealth that did nobody, including himself, any good.

By contrast, Paul interlaced churches in three different areas in the act of giving to one another. He wrote to the Corinthians about a collection being taken for the impoverished Jerusalem churches.[1] He reported how the churches in the region of Macedonia had already begun by making sacrificial contributions for their fellow Christians. Their ability to give even out of poverty came first from an internal focus not on self but on God and others: "They gave themselves first to the Lord and then by the will of God to us" (2 Corinthians 8:5). Giving themselves first to Christ meant acknowledging the source of life, provision and salvation. That opened them to the giving that creates communion with other believers.

Giving creates further ability to give. Two Deuteronomy passages indicate that being openhanded with the poor will lead to God's blessing on the work of our hands:

And the sojourner, the fatherless, and the widow, who are within your towns, shall come and eat and be filled, that the

LORD your God may bless you in all the work of your hands that you do. (Deuteronomy 14:29)

You shall not harden your heart or shut your hand against your poor brother, but you shall open your hand to him and lend him sufficient for his need, whatever it may be. . . . You shall give to him freely . . . because for this the LORD your God will bless you in all your work and in all that you undertake. (Deuteronomy 15:7-10)

The Hebrews with land that produced harvests were to share with those who did not have means to get their own food. Notice the flow here: God had already blessed the landowners with a good crop. But when they filled the hungry with food, God would go on to bless further the labor they put into their farms.

Does this mean no Hebrew farmer who was generous with the poor would never see crops destroyed by hail or drought? Would he always have bumper harvests? Of course not. But giving does indeed change us. It increases our capacity to be thankful and enjoy what we have. It also enables us to bless others even more. Paul communicated this as he wrote,

The point is this: whoever sows sparingly will also reap sparingly, and whoever sows bountifully will also reap bountifully. Each one must give as he has decided in his heart, not reluctantly or under compulsion, for God loves a cheerful giver. And God is able to make all grace abound to you, so that having all sufficiency in all things at all times, you may abound in every good work. . . .

He who supplies seed to the sower and bread for food will supply and multiply your seed for sowing and increase the harvest of your righteousness. You will be enriched in every way to be generous in every way, which through us will produce thanksgiving to God. (2 Corinthians 9:6-8, 10-11)

A little bit of giving keeps us in a reduced blessing mode. Generous giving opens us to participate more and more in what God is up to in the world. He supplies our needs when we are not hoarding but sharing. And he pours through more in order that we may have the joy of doing more to bless others. Something as seemingly nonspiritual as giving money takes us right to the heart of our God. In the context of a discussion about financial collection, Paul makes one of his great theological statements about Jesus: "For you know the grace of our Lord Jesus Christ, that though he was rich, yet for your sake he became poor, so that you by his poverty might become rich" (2 Corinthians 8:9). The Son of God emptied himself to make us rich with salvation and grace. He gave up everything for our sake, all the way to losing what was most precious, his sense of intimacy with his Father, during his forsakenness on the cross. But when he rose, he received back everything. As he told his disciples, "All authority in heaven and on earth has been given to me" (Matthew 28:18). His is the name that is above all names (Philippians 2:9). From such an exalted position, when all tribute is due to him, Jesus continues to give. He makes us rich as he pours out his Spirit on more and more people, pulling them within his blessing sphere. Jesus remains in the blessing flow of giving. Astoundingly, we show forth this great truth with effective power through the way we give our money.

Ripple Effect

Paul went on to explain how the Corinthian contribution to relieve the Jerusalem believers would do much more than alleviate physical want:

> For the ministry of this service is not only supplying the needs of the saints but is also overflowing in many thanksgivings to God. By their approval of this service, they will

glorify God because of your submission flowing from your confession of the gospel of Christ, and the generosity of your contribution for them and for all others, while they long for you and pray for you, because of the surpassing grace of God upon you. Thanks be to God for his inexpressible gift! (2 Corinthians 9:12-15)

Look how the blessing life worked out: 1) The Corinthians confessed the truth of the gospel. That is, they received the blessing of restored communion with God through the work of Jesus Christ in the union created by the Spirit. 2) The Corinthians submitted to the claim of God on their lives. They became willing to bless God in return by learning and obeying his will. 3) The Corinthians would go on to extend financial blessing to the Christians in Jerusalem. 4) This act of blessing would cause Jerusalem believers to bless God even more. 5) The Jerusalem Christians would pray for God to bless the Corinthians for further service in blessing. 6) Pulling in an earlier passage, we see that the Corinthian giving would result in others giving to them should they have future need: "Your abundance at the present time should supply their need, so that their abundance may supply your need, that there may be fairness" (2 Corinthians 8:14).

Once engaged, the blessing life both interconnects participants and continues to ripple outward, furthering the gospel as the triune God re-blesses his lost world.

A Micro Example with Macro Rebound

Several of our elders meet early every Tuesday morning to pray and to study the passage for the next Sunday's sermon. During our focus on the blessing life, an elder came in bursting with a story. He had just stopped at a convenience store for a coffee and a bottle of water. There were several people ahead of him in line to pay. The man in front of him said, making what appeared to be small talk, "Isn't it a beautiful day, with the flowers beginning to come out and the air getting warmer?"

Our elder quipped back, "Sure, warm today and freezing tomorrow. That's Baton Rouge."

The man replied, "And thank God anyway!"

Our elder realized this was more than an idle conversation. "Yes," he said. "You're exactly right!" At this moment he looked up and noticed one of the workers behind the counter looking at him. They smiled at each other as a moment of understanding passed between them.

When he got to the front of the line, the employee moved to the register, purse in hand. "I'd like to buy your items," she said, looking at our elder and interrupting the cashier. My friend started to protest. He is quite obviously not impoverished. His business has prospered and he thanks God for it. A convenience store worker doesn't make a lot of money. His items could cost her half an hour's work. But then he realized that this was an important moment for her.

"Thank you," he said. "Where do you go to church?" They talked briefly about their churches, sharing a moment of fellowship. Then our elder, who has the gift of giving and just couldn't contain himself any longer, asked if she would make a donation to her church for him. He gave her twenty dollars and went on his way to our study.

Our elder couldn't wait to share how contagious blessing proved to be. A man in an early-morning coffee line took a complaint and turned it into public blessing of God. This open expression of faith created a point of connection between two believers from very different walks of life. But the one with less of the world's goods was moved to bless with a gift the one with more. In his surprised gratitude, he sent a blessing gift on its way out of the store to her church. Perhaps the ripple is still running! Giving—of praise or money, time or energy—creates opportunity for more giving.

God Funds

For the last twenty years I have been fairly bold in preaching about tithing. Rhonda and I saw our lives and finances change as we accepted the challenge to give back to God at least ten percent of what he gives to us. I don't believe you can make a direct correlation between tithing and getting blessed with a particular level of prosperity in return. There is no formula for how to make money off of giving to God. But I have talked to lots of people who are tithers and who come from all income levels. Not one has ever complained about giving too much. No one has ever felt any sense of want, even though they did not all, by any means, become rich as the world defines it. But they all report feeling abundantly blessed by God with everything they need for themselves and everything they need to keep giving.

When I first came to Baton Rouge and spoke of this during stewardship season, something clicked for one of our elders. He and his wife determined to create a "God fund." They put cash into the fund every month and then waited to see what God showed them to do. He had such joy as he told me about all that had happened. "It's God's money," he said. "But it's so much fun that he lets us be the ones who give it to others."

Blessing people through giving money is a fulfilling pleasure. Our level of income doesn't matter. The Macedonian churches gave out of their extreme poverty and were thrilled to do so. Others give out of great wealth. The point is to be in the blessing loop with our money in the same way we are with our praise, prayer, energy and time. Whether it's buying coffee for the person in line behind us or funding someone's seminary education, giving blesses others and blesses the giver with a great sense of participation in God's worldwide blessing project. Our Lord Jesus certainly knew this as he said, "It is more blessed to give than to receive" (Acts 20:35).

17

GETTING LINED UP WITH GOD

❧

*P*rayer is an integral part of the blessing life. We bless others through our prayers for them and, at the same time, our prayers open up opportunities for us to bless them directly. Prayer awakens us to see the ways God wants to bless others through us.

My friend and colleague Nancy Spiller recently took a young woman from our church to lunch. They had connected during a women's retreat and Nancy wanted to encourage her. The two met at a little restaurant next to an interior design office. Before lunch, Nancy prayed, "Lord, I want to bless her with encouragement. But I don't know her very well. I don't really know what to say. Please help me." As the meal progressed, the younger woman shared how frustrated she was. Once she had been married, working and living in another city. Now the marriage was over and she was living back home having trouble figuring out what she wanted to do for work.

Nancy asked, "So what do you really like to do?"

She replied, "Well, it's funny, but I really like helping people get organized. Closets, bedrooms and kitchens are my favorite."

Within minutes, the owner of the neighboring interior design firm walked into the restaurant. She knew Nancy and came right over to the table. Nancy had no idea this old friend had an office adjacent to the restaurant. Nancy introduced the two women. The interior designer asked, "So what do you do?"

The younger woman hesitated since she wasn't currently working. But Nancy chimed in, "She's a professional organizer!"

"Really? That's great. We're actually looking for someone to help us with that."

How many "coincidences" had to occur for that connection to be made? Nancy prayed for God to bless her lunchmate and to be a blessing to her. God answered. I don't know if the encounter actually led to a job, but I do know the young woman was inspired to believe she could work in the field suited to her gifts. The future was no longer closed but open to her.

That's the way prayer and blessing work together. It's not us dictating to God how he should bless someone and then we tell a great story about how God did just what we asked. Rather, we make ourselves available to participate in the blessing work of our loving heavenly Father. We ask God to bless and to use us to be a blessing. The joy is seeing the mysterious, it-could-only-be-God ways that he answers. Nancy offered herself in prayer. This heightened her ability to see when God was working, and she went on to participate in the blessing God orchestrated.

The Fullness of the Blessing of Christ

Amidst the majesty of the doctrine Paul writes in Romans, we also see an intimate personal side to this great apostle when he reveals his tender heart for the Christians in Rome. When we combine his words at the beginning and end of his letter with our knowledge from Acts about what actually happened, we see an amazing confluence of prayer and the blessing of God.

Paul opens his letter declaring how "constantly I remember you in my prayers at all times" (Romans 1:9-10). Within Paul's concern for the Roman Christians, he has a specific request: "that now at last by God's will the way may be opened for me to come to you" (Romans 1:10). Why is he entreating God to send him to Rome? So he can bless them with encouragement: "I long to see you so that I may impart to you some spiritual gift to make you strong" (Romans 1:11). And Paul knows that if God gets him there, he will be so in the flow of the blessing dynamic that he too will be blessed: "that you and I may be mutually encouraged by each other's faith" (Romans 1:12).

At the close of his letter, Paul invites the church into his prayers to be able to visit. He urges them "to join me in my struggle by praying to God for me . . . so that I may come to you with joy, by God's will, and in your company be refreshed" (Romans 15:30, 32). Together they will pray that Paul can escape persecution long enough to get up from Jerusalem to Rome. His desire is a blessing one: "I know that when I come to you, I will come in the full measure of the blessing of Christ" (Romans 15:29).

Paul had knowledge of the glories of God's love. He saw things no one had ever seen in the Scriptures. He knew that teaching the truth of the gospel would bring joyful transformation to his students. And he knew that face to face, in dialogue, is the way disciples are grown.

We get an idea of what he meant by "the full measure of the blessing of Christ" when we look at the opening prayer of his letter to the Ephesian church, where he fairly sings, "Praise be to the God and Father of our Lord Jesus Christ, who has blessed us in the heavenly realms with every spiritual blessing in Christ" (Ephesians 1:3). The passage drips with blessing! In Christ we have all God has to give us. Paul goes on to detail what these treasures are: to be holy and blameless before God, to be adopted in Christ as God's own children, to know ourselves chosen and accepted in Christ, to experience redemption from slavery to sin and forgiveness of sins committed, to be part of God's eternal plan to unite and renew all things in Christ (Ephesians 1:4-10). Paul's prayer to visit the Roman Christians has at its heart the desire to impart the inestimable treasure of discovering all we have in belonging to Christ Jesus.

Surely God would answer such a perfect prayer, right? Here is where the history recorded in Acts shows us something of the mysterious interplay between our prayers, God's answers and the blessing of others. For a long time it must have seemed to Paul that he would not be granted his heart's request. He did not escape persecution in Jerusalem. Instead he got arrested and a mob virulently demanded that the Roman authorities put him to death. Only Paul's assertion of his Roman citizenship saved him from a brutal flogging and certain execution, and the pagan Roman tribunal had to smuggle him out of town to save Paul from an ambush. Paul weathered accusations before official after official and bore witness to the truth of Jesus every time he was allowed to speak. Eventually he was placed as a prisoner on a ship bound for Rome! But even then he had to endure a violent storm at sea, shipwreck and months of delay.

Finally he arrived in Rome and, though still a prisoner, he got to live under "house arrest," having freedom to teach those who came to him for two years. Acts tells us that Paul did indeed bless and receive the blessing of encouragement from the Roman Christians for which he had prayed years before (Acts 28:15).

Paul and the Roman Christians received what they prayed for but not in the way they had anticipated. God answered with more suffering, uncertainty and anxiety for Paul than even he could have imagined. But he also provided more opportunity to witness to influential people than he ever could have dared to hope. In the end he found the believers in Rome and blessed them. He was not a free man for those two years and yet he was able to teach daily.

The way of blessing and prayer can be difficult and surprising, but as we persist we discover it to be ultimately fulfilling.

"I Got Your Back"

Graham Thompson's grandson was recently deployed to Afghanistan with the US Marine Corps. During one of our board meetings, Graham shared with his fellow elders how he and his daughter-in-law had been praying for Mac. "Merri Hope and I have been praying that God would send his angels to protect and encourage Mac during his tour of duty as a Marine in Afghanistan."

Graham said Mac got to call home only once every three weeks, when his turn came to use the satellite phone. He always seemed glad to hear the voices from home, but he never wanted to share any of his feelings or experiences from that bizarre, disturbing world. More than one young man has had his faith shattered during such a tour of duty. At one point Merri Hope asked her son, "Mac, are you aware that God sends his angels to watch over you?"

His reply was sadly matter-of-fact: "No, Mom, I'm not."

Mothers, though, don't give up easily. "Well, Mac, look for them," she said.

Graham went on to relay what happened to Mac soon after. Mac and another Marine went behind enemy lines to do reconnaissance. They endured harrowing danger. One night, still in enemy territory, Mac and his colleague found an indentation in the sand to hide in.

Later, the young man who had previously never shared his feelings about the war told his mother, "Mom, I never felt more afraid in my life, or more alone. I felt like I had nobody. I was as low as I've ever been. My buddy and I lay down back to back to keep warm. I looked up and decided I needed to pray. As I lay there in the desert looking up at the stars, I saw a meteor shower. There were more shooting stars than I'd ever seen. They came down one after another, so beautiful in the dark night. And then I knew God had actually been watching out for me. It's like he told me what we in the brotherhood of the Marines say to each other in the field all the time: 'Mac, I got your back.' He had been sending his angels. I understood then what you had been praying for me all along."

Prayers bless in more ways than we imagine. More than anything, Mac's parents and grandparents wanted the blessing of his safety. And this time they received that gift. But their deepest satisfaction is the blessing Mac received in discovering deep in his bones that God truly is with him all the time. That relationship makes him all right in the deepest sense of the world, even if one of the world's perils—abroad or at home—should strike him.

What Kind of World?

I rejoiced to hear that story. But also I couldn't help wondering how it interacted with Claire Wilson's story in the introduction to this book—Mac survived an enemy firestorm and then got safely home, while Van endured a dangerous training operation and then died driving back to see his parents. How does that figure? Was it some failure in the prayers of his parents? In chapter 3, we saw that Susie Tucker recovered from a vicious cancer but another woman did not. Were more people praying for one woman than the other? Or people with more faith?

That can't be it. Such a system would throw the entire burden back on us. It would make blessing available only to the "worthy." That's exactly the opposite of what people report who experience healing or protection. They don't feel like they earned it at all, either themselves or through their churches. They feel graced. They say they discovered God's faithfulness before they knew how things would work out, and that even if everything had gone wrong, they would still have blessed God for the sweetness of his loving presence.

Before they were thrown into the fiery furnace, the three friends of the prophet Daniel made a striking declaration. The pagan king demanded that they worship a statue of him or be killed. The young men replied, "If we are thrown into the blazing furnace, the God we serve is able to deliver us from it, and he will deliver us from Your Majesty's hand. But even if he does not, we want you to know, Your Majesty, that we will not serve your gods or worship the image of gold you have set up" (Daniel 3:17-18).

"But even if he does not . . . " Prayers for blessing protection, health, safety and prosperity are not always answered as we hope. The history of God's people shows that many went to their deaths for their faith. But the deeper blessing of knowing they lived and died in a world ruled by the God who gave his very life for them sustained them with a joy they would never trade.

A woman in our church has within the last three years endured breast cancer, the loss of her mother, acute facial pain and the stark decline of her husband to rapid-onset dementia. She has been smacked hard and often by life in this world and drained to exhaustion by the demands of care. Prayers for healing have not been answered as she wished. But she declares boldly, tearfully, "I wouldn't trade these last three years for anything. The closeness I feel to my husband, my church and especially to my God who sustains me is more precious than anything else." Her prayers and those of others have led not directly to what they asked for but to a communion of love so blessed that it seems the greater gift.

I realize that these thoughts and stories create at least three faith choices for us regarding prayer and blessing. For one, we can remain skeptical about people who report God's direct hand in the supposed signs of his blessing. We can be tempted to ascribe the blessing moment to people's experience and even their projection onto the world of events as responses to prayers. It's not heard to "psychologize" and therefore trivialize experiences like I've re-

ported here about Nancy and Mac. Or, second, we can behold trag-
edies such as the deaths of Van and the young blogger and simply
lose our faith. We can become cynics who declare that if these
people aren't blessed (as we have defined blessing in our prayers
for them) then our prayers are all a fantasy.

But third, we can choose to see a world full of wonders because
our blessing God remains involved with us. He who spoke the
golden thread through the Scriptures "I will be your God" continues to answer our blessing prayers through mysterious grace we
can only see with eyes of faith. My work as a pastor puts my face
in a lot of tragedy and suffering. It wears on me. But the truth that
has risen in my heart during these decades of ministry is actually a
joyful one. God's people eventually see his blessing love even
through suffering. As we keep praying, we see that he answers. Not
always as we wish, but always as advances his glory in the world
and his purpose in us. He gives us "grace to help in time of need"
(Hebrews 4:16). I've made a choice to expect to see his blessing
surprises in response to prayer. God's people report the wonders of
his love to me again and again. The choice to have faith that prayer
connects us to blessing, though it may be in ways we do not expect
or understand, makes all the difference.

Prayer and Community

I introduced you to Katy Cosby back in chapter 4. Her sister yanked
her out of the darkness by getting her into a treatment center when
her life had gone off the rails. The redemptive work of God came
full circle recently when Katy's sister went through a dramatic
crisis. Just a few days before her due date, Katy's sister, Stacie Price,
had to undergo an emergency Cesarean delivery of her second
child. The baby arrived in this daylight world with a heart that had
stopped beating. The medical team managed to restart his heart,
but the situation was critical. Little Calvin's organs began to shut

down and there seemed little hope. Doctors lowered his body temperature to give Calvin a slim chance to recover from the trauma. Katy, nearly finished with her nursing residency, jumped in the car and headed for Houston four hours away. There she became the information hub for the family. Relieving Stacie and her husband, Jesse, Katy coordinated family help, relayed information to relatives and our church, and updated us constantly on how to pray.

When I talked to Stacie during that first week, in spite of her intense focus on Calvin, she mentioned the wonder of seeing her sister performing such an amazing service. "To think where she was just a few years ago," Stacie said. "I knew I had to do something for her, but I never imagined that she would return the love to me in such a crucial way."

Meanwhile the body of Christ swung into action. With just a few hours' notice more than forty people showed up in our chapel on a Friday night to pray. Hundreds more prayed from afar. Emails, Facebook statuses and text messages lit up with prayers and encouragement. Church members went to visit and reported sweet times of prayer with the family. The Prices felt lifted up and sustained by our prayers. We all felt knit closer and close to their hearts.

Calvin leapt through one critical medical hurdle after another. Every meeting of our church, whether for worship, Bible study or business, lifted up the Price family. We knew that the fervency of our prayers did not guarantee the outcome we desired. But we also knew we were called to pray and our hearts would not allow us to turn from asking God for miracles and mercy. Could it possibly have been an accident that in a hospital as huge as the ones in Houston, with only two babies assigned per nurse in the neonatal unit, that the niece of Nancy (mentioned in the opening of this chapter) was assigned to Calvin? She got to put Calvin in the arms of his mother as she held him for the first time more than ten days after his birth. The faith of Stacie and Jesse blessed everyone who encountered them. And every believer who knew the couple constantly asked God's blessing grace for them. We saw remarkable healing occur. In the process we were all made more and more into one family in Christ.

Prayer unites God's people heart to heart. It opens us to see the myriad ways God is blessing us all the time. It reveals a world of wonders. Participants become closer to each other than even blood relatives. The blessing of the body of Christ is knit together in its sinews by prayer offered under the guidance of the Spirit.

Taking Others Up to the High Country

One summer when our children were young, we swapped houses and pulpits with a Scottish minister and his family. In Mallaig, a fishing village on the coast of the West Highlands, the church held a prayer meeting every Saturday night. One of the regular participants was a shepherd named Ewan. I'm a city boy and had never met someone with such a biblical profession. I remember how huge and strong Ewan's hands were. If he didn't know to show considerable restraint, he would have crushed my preacher hand. But when he prayed, Ewan was as gentle as one of his lambs. In fact, being with Ewan in prayer was like being taken on a journey up into the high hills off the coastland. He began slowly, thanking God for the blessings of provision through the week. But gradually Ewan took us higher and Scripture verses began to flow in his rich Highland accent. It was clear that while he walked with his sheep on long summer days Ewan also walked and talked with his God. It was apparent through this man's prayers that he was on familiar terms with Christ. Eventually he brought us to great heights of praise. I always felt that I had been taken up into heaven before we made our way back to earth interceding for others.

Twenty minutes was not an unusual amount of time for Ewan to pray. But he never rambled. He went somewhere with God, and we got to go along. The effect of such prayer was a powerful blessing on participants in the group. Ewan praised God, but he collected us and took us with him to the high country. It was as effective in my heart as if he had praying specifically for me. Blessing God blesses others.

More recently I experienced this kind of prayer in a more compact time frame. Dr. Michael Milton, the chancellor of my seminary, called me in my office. He was making contact with donors and alumni. We chatted for a few minutes about ministry in Baton Rouge and plans at the school. As it came time to close, he asked if he could pray for me. I expected a typical nice but brief blessing. Instead, Mike turned in prayer to the great blessing praises of the angels around the throne in Revelation. He blessed God with the words of Scripture as the means of interceding for me. I felt bathed in heavenly light. Taking me with him to the heavenly reality was a richer blessing even than specific intercessions for my ministry needs. By looking upward, beyond our earthly work, Mike united us in the Spirit, set our daily tasks on a higher plane and left me awash in God's glory. Prayer together when we bless God becomes a powerful blessing to others.

Next time you're in worship, try holding in your mind someone for whom you've been praying. Sing the words of praise to God robustly, but do it with the image of someone who needs God's care clearly in your mind. You'll find that you don't really need to tell God how to bless this person. Praising the Father, Son and Spirit while bringing someone with you in your heart becomes a powerful form of intercession.

Finally, I encourage you to work with the great benedictions at the end of each of the New Testament letters. These passages give us hearty words to link what we know of God to what we know of another person. They focus our prayers on the vision God has for the ones we love and even for the ones with whom we are at odds. Much like the blessing speech we considered in chapter 13, these benedictions make great prayers to send people in a note or email. For example, consider who comes to mind as needing you to pray this prayer from the conclusion of Romans: "May the God of hope fill you with all joy and peace in believing, so that by the power of the Holy Spirit you may abound in hope" (Romans 15:13). Now that you have prayed it, consider how you will write or say it aloud for that person. Living to bless means passing the blessing forward!

18

WHERE IT ALL LEADS

༄

$\mathcal{I}$ hope that you have been inspired throughout this journey. My prayer is that you indeed feel as if you have stepped into the life of the triune God who is even now extending his blessing across the globe. We have attempted to view the great biblical story of redemption through the lens of blessing. We have seen that the heart of the whole story can be told in blessing terms. All along we have attempted to a) receive the blessing of God as revealed in Scripture, b) return that blessing back to God in praise and then c) reflect that blessing love to others as part of Christ's mission to the world.

Throughout we have discovered that the deep meaning of blessing in the Bible is communion with God and one another. The phrase that beats like a strong heart through the whole story is "I will be your God and you will be my people." God wants to be in a life-giving relationship with us. So much so that from before eternity, the triune God determined to make this communion possible in spite of the sin we would in our free will inevitably choose. The Father sent the Son to remake our humanity so that, joined to him by the Holy Spirit, we might be taken up into the life of God.

When we know that, we discover that the grand, joyous purpose of our lives on this earth is to participate in extending that blessing to all we can.

The final vision comes from Revelation 21. The garden of communion will be restored as a city teeming with people. God will have his desire fulfilled. He will dwell with us in a joyous fellowship of love. Consider this passage in terms of the blessing life we have explored:

> Then I saw a new heaven and a new earth, for the first heaven and the first earth had passed away, and the sea was no more. And I saw the holy city, new Jerusalem, coming down out of heaven from God, prepared as a bride adorned for her husband. And I heard a loud voice from the throne saying, "Behold, the dwelling place of God is with man. He will dwell with them, and they will be his people, and God himself will be with them as their God. He will wipe away every tear from their eyes, and death shall be no more, neither shall there be mourning, nor crying, nor pain anymore, for the former things have passed away."
>
> And he who was seated on the throne said, "Behold, I am making all things new." Also he said, "Write this down, for these words are trustworthy and true." And he said to me, "It is done! I am the Alpha and the Omega, the beginning and the end. To the thirsty I will give from the spring of the water of life without payment. The one who conquers will have this heritage, and I will be his God and he will be my son. But as for the cowardly, the faithless, the detestable, as for murderers, the sexually immoral, sorcerers, idolaters, and all liars, their portion will be in the lake that burns with fire and sulfur, which is the second death." (Revelation 21:1-8)

I thrill to the hope of the new heaven and the new earth. The garden lost will be the garden city regained. He who has remade our humanity will make the entire creation new. No more loss. No more futility of falling apart. Our deep soul thirst will be assuaged with joy. Revelation 22:1-5 expands this vision with more information. The tree of life, once guarded from us, will be in the midst of that city, its fruit available for everyone there. Its leaves will create the healing of the nations as it grows astride the river of the water of life. The triune God himself will be the light of that city. We will see him face to face, no longer separated by anything. The vision makes me ache for its beauty.

But it also disturbs me. For this magnificent vision ends with a rather dire warning: "Outside are the dogs and sorcerers and the sexually immoral and murderers and idolaters, and everyone who loves and practices falsehood" (Revelation 22:15). I am chilled to the soul by this sentence. For I, in my heart and too often in my practice, am the liar, the idolater, the faithless, the detestable. No sin, no matter how heinous, is beyond my reach. Is there nothing but eternal death awaiting me?

But then I read more closely. The warning is to those who choose to remain in the sin their hearts generate rather than give over their hearts to the one who makes all things new. The terror is for those who will prefer the old Adam to the new and not, in their pride, ever cry out that life on our own does not, can never, work.

I take my place not with the self-satisfied, then, but with the thirsty. I want to drink from the river of the water of life. I have nothing with which I can pay. No strength to be a conqueror. No hope except that the Alpha and Omega has spoken to me. He will be my Father and I his true son. In Christ. Only in Christ. Ever in Christ.

The Palimpsest of the Blessing Life

My daughter recently taught me a word from the world of art: *palimpsest*. A palimpsest is a canvas or wall with more than one painting on it, or a parchment manuscript written on more than once. We see in ancient churches how sometimes the original fresco on a wall begins to come through the painting on the surface. Some very valuable art has been discovered when the presenting painting has given way to the original. In a palimpsest, what is underlying shows through as the surface is examined closely. In their class discussions, my daughter and her fellow students use the word *palimpsest* more broadly to refer to the whole exploration of trying to find the deeper meaning rising through a work of literature or theology.

I've spent the last several years intensely studying the theme of blessing in Scripture. Along the way I've realized that the blessing life is a palimpsest. Something arises from participating in the blessing story God is telling—joy. The joy of deep communion with the God who made us to relate to him. The joy of connecting to others in blessing love. When we engage in the blessing life, indwelling the blessing story of God and living it out, joy emerges in our lives.

I offer the unfamiliar word *palimpsest* because it articulates the reality of how blessing and joy go together. I cannot promise a one-to-one connection between joy and the blessing life. We cannot say, "Bless God in these words according to this specific blessing plan and you will be joyful. Bless others with these ten easy steps and happiness will be yours." God doesn't work that way. He does not allow his blessing love to be packaged in a formula that we market and control. The triune God of grace is after, as he has been since the world was made, a continuing, real relationship of love with each of us. When we pursue daily such communion with him through Christ, joy arises that ever surprises and endures, even through the hardest of times.

I know this as a personal fact. In recent years both my parents passed away. During a hurricane one tree crashed through our bedroom while another destroyed our garage and two cars. A family member went through a serious depression. We got swindled out of a lot of money. I went through a cancer scare and then a serious back injury.

But none of those stole my joy. Actually, each of those situations drove me to seek Jesus. And he showed up. He kept me company during long nights. He gave me peace during impossible decisions. We knew deep in our bones that he would take care of us. He connected us to other people with a depth we'd never known. The hard times were just that—hard! But, strangely, on reflection I realize I have never had more joy in my life. Because I know the blessing of communion with Christ.

When we leave off trying to manage our own lives and receive deeply the lordship of Jesus Christ, the incarnate blessing of God, we enter the blessing dynamic of communion with God and deepening love toward others. We join God's massive re-blessing project in the world. And along the way, joy arises in our lives.

We are traveling to the land where there is no more dying, no more crying but life everlasting in communion as the bride with her bridegroom. This will be the blessedness for which we yearn. Along the way, we are living to bless. We invite a lost world into the journey of the blessing life. I'm so glad you joined me for these pages, and I hope I encouraged you as pilgrims on the way.

Now, as the LORD, the one true God, who is Father, Son and Holy Spirit, blesses you, shines his face upon you and keeps you in his grace, may I add the benediction of Jude:

> To those who are called, beloved in God the Father and kept for Jesus Christ: May mercy, peace, and love be multiplied to you. (Jude 1-2)

Amen.

Next Steps

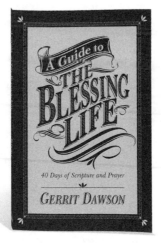

A Guide to The Blessing Life

The companion from InterVarsity Press to *The Blessing Life* gives you forty days of Bible readings in each category of the blessing dynamic: receiving, returning and reflecting the blessing love of God.

Print ISBN: 978-0-8308-3752-6
Digital ISBN: 978-0-8308-9560-1

Also Available

A project based on this much research necessarily leaves a lot of material on the cutting room floor. So I've got nearly one hundred more pages of free material for you! Visit www.fpcbr.org and click on The Blessing Life tab. There you'll find a small group discussion guide, concrete suggestions for daily blessing others, ancient blessing praises from the church fathers, and tons of material on the biblical story and theology underlying the blessing life.

FURTHER READING

❦

Austell, Robert M., Jr. *The Breadth of Worship: Eight Studies on Worship in the Scriptures*. Raleigh, NC: Lulu, 2010.

Dictionary of Biblical Imagery. Edited by Leland Ryken, James C. Wilhoit and Tremper Longman III. Downers Grove, IL: InterVarsity Press, 1998.

Hegg, Tim. "The Priestly Blessing." *Bikurie Zion*, 2001. www.torahresource.com/EnglishArticles/Aaronic%20Ben.pdf.

Horton, Michael. *God of Promise: Introducing Covenant Theology*. Grand Rapids: Baker Books, 2006.

Kapic, Kelly M. "Receiving Christ's Priestly Benediction: A Biblical, Historical, and Theological Exploration of Luke 24:50-53." *Westminster Journal of Theology* 65 (2005): 247-60.

Kapic, Kelly M., with Justin Borger. *God So Loved, He Gave: Entering the Movement of Divine Generosity*. Grand Rapids: Zondervan, 2010.

Pitre, Brant. *Jesus and the Jewish Roots of the Eucharist: Unlocking the Secrets of the Last Supper*. New York: Doubleday, 2011.

Ratzinger, Joseph (Pope Benedict XVI). *Jesus of Nazareth, Part Two. Holy Week: From the Entrance into Jerusalem to the Resurrection*. San Francisco: Ignatius Press, 2011.

Spangler, Ann, and Lois Tverberg. *Sitting at the Feet of Rabbi Jesus: How the Jewishness of Jesus Can Transform Your Faith*. Grand Rapids: Zondervan, 2009.

Waltke, Bruce, with Cathi J. Fredericks. *Genesis: A Commentary*. Grand Rapids: Zondervan, 2001.

Westermann, Claus. *Blessing in the Bible and the Life of the Church*. Translated by Keith Crim. Philadelphia: Fortress, 1978.

ACKNOWLEDGMENTS

I'd like to thank the companions who've been walking these blessing paths with me. The congregation and staff of the First Presbyterian Church of Baton Rouge have always been game for an adventure of knowing our Lord Jesus, trusting me and coming with me through every text. In particular, the elders in our Tuesday morning Bible study have been great exploring partners. I knew it would change my life to learn to get up that early, but I never could have dreamed of how much your faith, love, dedication, knowledge and interest in the Word would shape me so powerfully.

I rejoice, too, in friends and colleagues such as Tim Hatcher, Chuck and Mitzi Barber, Hank Mills, Mary Willson, Alec Flynt and others who studied blessing with me. You have a passion for Christ and his Word that is infectious. Katie Robinson has been a great help with images and layout, and my assistant Jaci Gaspard has served in a thousand ways. I'm grateful for all the extraordinary believers who have shared their blessing stories with me and allowed God to be glorified in their telling. Dearly beloved Rhonda, thank you for your faith that sustains: faith in the Lord Jesus and faith in me. I get nowhere without you.

I am particularly grateful to the congregation for the gift of a sabbatical leave in the summer of 2011 so that I could pull this manuscript together while at Fairlight Cottage in Brevard, North Carolina. Finally, across the centuries, I'd like humbly to take up the words of my brother in Christ from A.D. 400. At the end of his *Hymns for the Christian's Day*, Prudentius wrote,

> Lo in the palace of the King of kings
> I play the earthen pitcher's humble part;
> Yet to have done him meanest service brings
> A thrill of rapture to my thankful heart:
> What e'er the end, this thought will joy afford,
> My lips have sung the praises of my Lord.

NOTES

⟨✦⟩

Chapter 1

[1] The German scholar Claus Westermann has explored in detail the layers of meaning in God's blessing in his *Blessing in the Bible and the Life of the Church* (Philadelphia: Fortress, 1978), see especially p. 18.

[2] Larry Crabb, *Inside Out* (Colorado Springs, CO: NavPress, 1988), paraphrased from p. 74.

[3] In many English translations of the Old Testament, including the ESV used here, we find the name of God given in all capital letters as LORD. This translates the Hebrew word YHWH, which means "I am who I am." This is the unique name for our God disclosed to Moses. That's why you will see LORD in the OT quotations and occasionally in my text as well. By it I mean the one true God who would be revealed as Father, Son and Holy Spirit.

[4] John Updike, "Seven Stanzas at Easter," *Telephone Poles and Other Poems* (New York: Alfred A. Knopf, 1963), no. 72.

[5] The blog site from which this story was gleaned has been taken down, so I have worked from my transcripts from 2009. Diligent efforts to reach the family have been unsucessful.

Chapter 4

[1] My friend Dawn Eden uncovered this insight from history, especially in relation to the Ignatian prayer "Take, O Lord, and receive all my liberty, my memory, my understanding and my whole will," in her fine book *My Peace I Give You: Healing Sexual Wounds with the Help of the Saints* (Notre Dame, IN: Ave Maria Press, 2012), p. 20.

[2] Thanks to my friend Mitzi Barber, a great Hebrew student, for her enthusiasm for the striking image of the Creator God kneeling to bless his frail children. See also Tim Hegg, "The Priestly Blessing," *Bikurie Zion*, 2001, p. 4, www .torahresource.com/EnglishArticles/Aaronic%20Ben.pdf.

Chapter 5

[1] George Herbert, "Providence," *George Herbert: The Complete Poems*, ed. John Tobin (New York: Penquin Books, 1991), p. 108.

[2]W. C. Smith, "Immortal, Invisible, God Only Wise," *The Hymnal 1940* (New York: Church Hymnal Corporation, 1940), 301.

[3]Thomas O. Chisholm, "Great Is Thy Faithfulness," *Trinity Hymnal* (Suwanee, GA: Great Commission Publications, 1990), 32.

Chapter 6

[1]Michael Horton stands in a long tradition of those who call this the "covenant of redemption." Before the world began, the persons of the triune God determined and committed themselves to this plan of salvation. See *God of Promise: Introducing Covenant Theology* (Grand Rapids: Baker Books, 2006), pp. 78-82.

[2]Prudentius, *The Hymns of Prudentius*, trans. R. Martin Pope (London: J. M. Dent and Co., 1905), p. 3.

[3]Ibid., p. 5.

[4]Prudentius, "Hymn for All Hours," trans. John Mason Neale, *Hymns Ancient and Modern* (London: William Clowes and Sons, 1922), 56.

Chapter 7

[1]Paul Hobbs, "God on a Stick," *Alternative Worship*, ed. Jonny Baker and Doug Gay (Grand Rapids: Baker, 2004), p. 104.

Chapter 8

[1]"Creator of the Stars of Night," sixth- or seventh-century Latin hymn, trans. J. M. Neale, *The Hymnal Noted* (London: J. Masters & Co., 1851), pp. 33-34.

[2]Thomas Torrance, "Preaching Christ Today," in *A Passion for Christ*, ed. Gerrit Dawson and Jock Stein (Edinburgh: Handsel, 1999), p. 13.

[3]Prudentius, *The Hymns of Prudentius*, trans. R. Martin Pope (London: J. M. Dent, 1905), p. 68.

Chapter 9

[1]Edward Shillito, "Jesus of the Scars," in James Dalton Morrison, ed., *Masterpieces of Religious Verse* (New York: Harper Brothers, 1958), p. 235.

Chapter 10

[1]Gerrit Scott Dawson, *Jesus Ascended: The Meaning of Christ's Continuing Incarnation* (London: T & T Clark, 2004).

[2]As quoted in Kelly Kapic, "Receiving Christ's Priestly Benediction: A Biblical, Historical, and Theological Exploration of Luke 24:50-53," *Westminster Journal of Theology* 67 (2005): 259.

[3]Joseph Ratzinger (Pope Benedict XVI), *Jesus of Nazareth, Pt. 2. Holy Week: From Entrance into Jerusalem to the Resurrection* (San Francisco: Ignatius Press, 2011), pp. 292-93.

[4]Joseph Ratzinger, "The Beginning of a New Nearness," in *Images of Hope* (San Franscisco: Ignatius, 1997), p. 56.

[5]Ibid., pp. 57-9.

[6]Kapic, "Receiving Christ's Priestly Benediction," p. 252.

Chapter 12
[1]This is the theme phrase for the magnificent Bethel Bible Series, based on Genesis 12:3. The Bethel Series (Waunatee, WI: 1962). See also bethelseries .com.
[2]Presbyterian pastor Glenn Parkinson has an excellent book on how effective Christians can be in blessing rather than condemning our post-Christian culture: *Like the Stars* (New York: iUniverse, 2004).

Chapter 13
[1]Portions of this chapter appeared previously in my article "Blessing Speech," *Weavings: A Journal of the Christian Spiritual Life* 27 (January 2011): 6-11.
[2]This gleaning was part of God's provision for the poor in Israel. God's people left the edges of the fields and the stalks that were dropped for those who came along behind: "When you reap your harvest in your field and forget a sheaf in the field, you shall not go back to get it. It shall be for the sojourner, the fatherless, and the widow, that the LORD your God may bless you in all the work of your hands" (Deuteronomy 24:19).
[3]Bill Gothard, *The Power of Spoken Blessings* (Colorado Springs, CO: Multnomah, 2004), pp. 18-19.
[4]Ibid., p. 38.

Chapter 14
[1]Dan Allender, *The Wounded Heart* (Colorado Springs, CO: NavPress, 1992), pp. 215-225.

Chapter 15
[1]*The Book of Common Prayer* (New York: The Church Hymnal Corporation and Seabury Press, 1979), p. 483.
[2]Quotations from Bill Glass, "The Power of Blessing" (Dallas: Champions for Life, 2010), audio recording. See www.BillGlass.org.
[3]Discover more about these examples: Dan Cruver's Together for Adoption website, www.togetherforadoption.com, and his book *Reclaiming Adoption: Missional Living Through Rediscovery of Abba Father* (Adelphi, MD: Cruciform, 2011); Jill Rigby's Manners of the Heart website (www.mannersofthe heart.org) and her book *Raising Respectful Children in a Disrepectful World* (New York: Howard Books/Division of Simon & Schuster, 2006, 2013); Threads of Love (www.threadsoflove.com) and Nancy Zito's Gardere Community Christian School (www.gardereschool.com).

Chapter 16
[1]Kelly Kapic has an excellent look at the importance of the collection in *God So Loved He Gave: Entering the Movement of Divine Generosity* (Grand Rapids: Zondervan, 2010), pp. 204-9.

IMAGE CREDITS

❧

SCRIPTURE INDEX